BECOME A
COACH
LEADER

ONE CONVERSATION AT A TIME

**Learn to Engage in Crucial Conversations
to Build Loyalty, Trust and Connection**

Barb Pierce, BEng, MBA, PCC

Library and Archives Canada Cataloguing in Publication
Pierce, Barbara A.
Become a coach leader - one conversation at a time - learn to engage in crucial conversations to build loyalty, trust and connection by Barb Pierce

Includes index.
Also issued in electronic format.
ISBN 978-0-9920565-0-6

Editing by Abby Griffith
Book cover by Janet Pashleigh
Printed in the USA

Published by:
Coaching Horizons
26 Evelyn St.
Almonte, Ontario
K0A 1A0
www.coachinghorizons.ca

CONTENTS

FOREWORD

The world of professional coaching began emerging in the mid to late 1980s as the powerhouse CEOs of America's largest corporations stepped aside to make way for the next generation. These CEOs stayed on to "coach" their successors, borrowing the term from the worlds of college and professional sports. What they were actually doing was mentoring these successors, passing along the wisdom gained through a lifetime of leadership. Perhaps they chose the term "coach" because it sounded much more macho than "mentor", yet more likely it was because the sports coaching model was a widely understood adult relationship.

As this idea of "coaching" moved beyond the upper echelons of corporate America and began taking root in everyday living, it has slowly but surely evolved into the profession it is becoming today. Along the way, threads of concepts like positive psychology, appreciative inquiry, emotional intelligence and Socratic questioning have been woven into the practice of coaching.

Professional organizations such as the International Coaching Federation (ICF) as well as others have defined coaching as a separate and distinct modality and philosophy from the athletic model originally adopted. These definitions assert that the client is whole, capable and resourceful as well as the "expert" in his/her life and work; that the client holds the keys to their dreams, goals and aspirations and is completely able to utilize those keys to open any door.

In addition to clarifying the definition of coaching, these organizations have also identified and set forth ethics, standards, skill sets and behaviors that clearly distinguish the professional coach from professionals such as consultants, mentors, counselors and therapists.

Working within these defined guidelines and frameworks, the coach employs the professional coaching skill set and process to ask questions that elicit answers to client situations from within the client's own inherent wisdom. Within an atmosphere of non-judgment, the coach also employs his/her cultivated *rapid cognition*[1] and copious curiosity to allow both coach and client to tap into the realms beyond anything either currently knows, what Malcolm Gladwell refers to as the *adaptive unconscious*[2].

Whether you are someone interested in becoming a professional coach, or someone who wishes to add a coaching approach to your work and lifestyle, in this work by accomplished coach and experienced coach trainer Barb Pierce you gain a "peek behind the curtain" to grasp the basic skills of coaching.

Through conversational overviews of globally accepted coaching concepts coupled with transcripts of real-life coaching conversations to illustrate them, Barb provides you with a simple roadmap to develop your capabilities and cultivate a coaching approach to engaging in important conversations with others.

By practicing the exercises included here, you can stimulate within you an ever-deepening engagement in the powerful process of coaching. I believe you'll discover that you can lead and live even more effectively by engaging with others in conversations that provide collaboration for deeper self-awareness and inspired action. I wish you many profound experiences in coaching!

Amoráh Ross,
ICF Master Certified Coach & Certified Mentor Coach
www.amorah.com

---

1   Gladwell, Malcolm, Blink - The Power of Thinking Without Thinking, NY NY, Back Bay Books / Little, Brown and Company Hachette Book Group, 2005.
2   Gladwell, Malcolm, Blink - The Power of Thinking Without Thinking, NY NY, Back Bay Books / Little, Brown and Company Hachette Book Group, 2005.

ACKNOWLEDGMENTS

I would like to acknowledge and thank:

My family, Rob, Liam, Matthew and Emily Pierce. Thank you all for supporting the writing process which sometimes meant an absent mother, a messy house and packaged dinners. With three children and a husband, I was fortunate enough to be provided with numerous opportunities to refine my understandings about the coaching mindset throughout the writing process.

John Sweetnam, my Coaching Navigator business partner and friend. John is the founding partner of Coaching Navigator and the creator of the CARA process. John is a lifetime learner and was a key originator of many of the ideas and concepts in this book.

My Royal Roads University Graduate Certificate in Executive Coaching instructors: Alison Hendren, MCC, Carollyne Conlinn, MCC, Scott Richardson, MCC and Marjorie Busse, MCC. You have created a wonderful coaching program, and my coaching improved tremendously during the year I spent with you.

My coach and friend, Sandra Bourdeau. You are a kind-hearted and wonderful person, and it was a joy to work with you.

My mentor coach, Amorah Ross. You are a masterful coach and inspired many of the ideas in this book.

My book mentor, Roger Ellerton. Thank you for sharing your wisdom and experience in publishing educational books.

My editor, Abby Griffith. It was a pleasure to work with you. You are a natural at applying the appreciative inquiry approach — even before you knew what it was.

My graphic designer, Janet Pashleigh. Thank you for laying out the chapters. I love your clean designs and how easy it is to convey my ideas to you even though we live across the country from each other.

My yoga teachers, Yogrishi Vishvketu and Chetana Panwar. I have learned so much about connecting with my body, emotions, intuition, energy and spirit through your teachings.

My friends and colleagues who kindly read through all or part of the drafts, or contributed their own stories: Rob Pierce, Danielle Vachon, Sarah Wall, Sandra Bourdeau, John Sweetnam, Mary Biggs, Peter Frauley, Sandy Heron, Walt Stevenson, Mike Wlotzki, Reta Currie, Diane Colbeck and Linda Hardham.

INTRODUCTION

I became passionate about coaching in 1998 when I had the opportunity to work with a coach during a challenging time in my life. It was a busy year that marked many transitions for me. I had recently returned to work after having my first child, retired from the military after 13 years of service and moved from the suburbs to downtown Calgary.

I felt guilty about dropping off my infant at daycare and bewildered about how to be a leader in a non-military environment. I knew that I was more authoritative than my co-workers were accustomed to, yet I did not know how to adjust my leadership style, or how to fit in better with this new culture. While my organizational skills were appreciated and encouraged, I was initiating more changes than the organization could handle. I was getting some push-back. On the homefront, we had new financial pressures with a more expensive house. All in all, I was facing more changes than I was equipped to handle. It was time to ask for help.

Fortunately, the company that I was working with had a standing relationship with a coach who specialized in communications excellence. Working with her helped me get clear on what was wrong and what I needed to do about it. My coach then supported me through the process of identifying, and asking for, what I needed.

I won't say that working with a coach was easy — it wasn't. I was not accustomed to being honest and clear with my requests. Through the coaching process, I discovered not only how much I was lacking in self-awareness, but also how much I ignored my intuition in favor of how I thought I was *supposed* to behave. It's funny how that can backfire. People prefer authenticity. By behaving the way I thought I should be acting, I had lost myself in the process.

A couple of kids later and a year of coach training under my belt, I was diagnosed with stage-4 lymphoma. This turned out to be the biggest challenge that I had faced so far in my life. I feared for my life and the possibility of leaving my children without a mother. It forced me take a close look at what I had created and what behaviours I had condoned. Most importantly, it led me to acknowledge and do something about the anger that I had been carrying over from my childhood. The experience also highlighted my less than adequate communications skills and low self-esteem. During my treatment and healing, I signed up for intensive coaching, Neuro-Linguistic Programming (NLP) and hypnosis courses, during which I was able to focus inward on letting go of unhelpful behavior patterns while building up my personal resources.

The cancer turned out to be one of the best things for me (although it really sucked at the time). It woke me up to new possibilities. I started living life more fully and boldly. I lowered my defenses and became more clear about who I am, what I truly wanted out of life and how to ask for it. I became more courageous, more focused and more willing to trust, and act on, my intuition.

Fifteen years after my first coach experience, I continue to face situations that are beyond my current capabilities. I work with a coach to get through these situations more peacefully, more quickly and with outcomes that are in alignment with my beliefs and values. I now find it much easier to make decisions that support my health and well-being.

WHY THE COACH APPROACH?

Coaching skills allow you to connect with others more deeply and more intimately; this creates a foundation on which to engage in conversations that resolve challenges and achieve results without blame. Coaching skills help you to discover what is important to others and allow you to channel this knowledge in ways that propel both the individual and the organization forward. In coaching conversations, people are encouraged to take calculated risks.

In many cases, people learn coaching skills to support their leadership role rather than to become full-time professional coaches. This book is designed for leaders who want to incorporate a simple, strength-based coaching process into their leadership toolbox. This includes:

- Coaches who want to deepen the coaching experience by incorporating:
  - Neuro-Linguistic Programming
  - Somatics
  - Appreciative Inquiry
- Leaders and managers who want to lead in a collaborative and open environment
- Therapists, social workers and counselors who want to incorporate coaching skills into their practices
- Organizational Development and HR professionals
- Teachers and school principals who want to bring out the best in their students
- Sales managers who want to increase their performance
- Facilitators and conflict resolution specialists who want to hone the unique art of conversational change
- Parents who want to connect better with their children

HOW THE COACH APPROACH HAS HELPED ME

One of the biggest benefits I've noticed from learning the coach approach is that I can now engage in difficult conversations before they become explosive. In most cases, having these conversations early on has resulted in greater trust and stronger connections. Coach skills have proved to be invaluable both at work and at home. At work, I am much more confident in dealing with conflict. I can now approach difficult conversations with ease and confidence. I no longer avoid initiating challenging conversations. Instead, I take the time to connect with each of the team members, learn what is important to them and create an atmosphere of openness and trust. When things go wrong, there is already a foundation of respect, which frees us to focus on the solution — not the person who made the mistake.

At home, the coach approach has helped me to be much calmer and more hopeful in the face of teen and pre-teen madness. I don't profess to be a perfect parent, but I believe that I am giving my children the skills and opportunities to become better decision makers. I have let them make difficult decisions, I have let them make bad decisions, and I have let them fail. Sometimes it was hard (and heartbreaking) to watch my children deal with the outcomes of their poor decisions, but I know that it will make them stronger in the end.

WHAT IS UNIQUE ABOUT OUR APPROACH?

We offer a simple, logical and easy-to-understand approach to productive conversations using the proven 4-step CARA coaching model. This process can be incorporated into your current leadership style and is flexible enough to be used fluidly in any conversation. You will not be bound by pre-determined questions or a rigid process. The principles are straightforward, easy to understand and they enable you to engage in challenging and authentic conversations.

At Coaching Navigator, our leadership coaching approach is based on the appreciative inquiry (AI) model. In a nutshell, AI is a method of communicating in which the focus is on the desired result rather than on the problem that led to the discussion. The process allows you to learn from past experiences but does not keep you trapped in negative associations.

The CARA model, developed at Coaching Navigator, builds on the excellence of Neuro-Linguistic Programming (NLP) — an approach to change based on creating new neural pathways in the brain. NLP explores the interaction between mind (neuro), language (linguistic) and behaviors (programming).

Finally, new coaches sometimes rely on logical thinking, and ignore intangibles like intuition and emotions. This approach can severely limit your capacity to learn, grow and achieve excellence. It also hinders your ability to connect with and motivate others. This book will help you to identify and integrate your feelings, intuition and emotions, and then translate them into conversations and decisions — even in a business setting. You will also learn techniques to calm yourself before, during and after challenging conversations to maintain your resourcefulness. This is called centering.

HOW TO USE THIS BOOK

The book begins with an overview of coaching, appreciative inquiry and somatics. You will learn the 4-step CARA coaching process that will give you the tools to engage in any conversation with confidence. Finally, you will learn how to integrate coaching skills into your leadership toolbox — in a way that is authentic for you. Each chapter includes opportunities to reflect on what you have learned, exercises to help you integrate these lessons into your everyday life, and sample coaching discussions to give you a feel for the flow of a coaching conversation. To maximize your results, start implementing these concepts right away.

How This Book is Organized

Part 1 - The Fundamentals

Chapter 1- Introduction to Coaching and the CARA Process

This chapter focuses on defining leadership coaching, how coaching is incorporated into the leadership toolbox, and the basic principles of coaching conversations. The chapter also introduces the 4-step CARA coaching model.

Chapter 2 - Appreciative Inquiry

This chapter focuses on the principles of Appreciative Inquiry (AI) and how to incorporate these concepts into your leadership coaching. You learn what AI is, the five principles of AI, and the 4-D Cycle — a simple series of steps to facilitate a change using AI.

Chapter 3 - Somatic Coaching

This chapter focuses on helping you create more authentic connections with others by becoming attuned to your intuition, feelings and emotions, as well as those of others. You will also learn about the five levels in which change can take place and discover questions to help catalyze change at each of these layers.

Part 2 - The 4-Step CARA Model

Chapter 4 - Connection

This chapter focuses on the Connection step of the CARA process. You will learn about proactive steps you can take to promote healthy connections with others. This helps you improve your relationships both at work and at home. You will also learn how to create a safe environment for discussions, how to center yourself before, during and after coaching meetings and how to develop skills to help you notice clues offered by body language, tone of voice and word choice.

Chapter 5 - Awareness

This chapter focuses on the Awareness step of the CARA process. You will learn how to negotiate a clear meeting agreement to maximize efficiency, as well as active listening skills to help you guide the coachee towards awareness of her topic.

Chapter 6 - Resources

This chapter focuses on the Resources step of the CARA process. You will learn how to lead your coachee to a positive frame of mind and how to use powerful questions to help her more fully explore her resources. You will also learn when to use descriptive questions vs. creative questions to maximize your results.

Chapter 7 - Action

This chapter focuses on the Action step of the CARA process. You learn the accountability sequence necessary to help your coachee create and sustain forward movement.

PART 3 - BECOME A COACH LEADER

Chapter 8 - Masterful Performance Feedback

This chapter focuses on how to deliver masterful performance feedback using the CARA process. You learn the difference between constructive criticism and constructive feedback, and how to set up a feedback conversation that strengthens relationships and creates a growth opportunity for the recipient of the feedback.

Chapter 9 - Uncovering Your Employees' Values, Beliefs and Motivations

This chapter teaches you the skills to help you elicit your coachees' values and beliefs. You can then use this information to ensure that your coachees' development plans are in alignment with what is important to them.

Chapter 10 - Acknowledgment

This chapter focuses on helping you understand the difference between acknowledgment and praise, and gives you tips on how to incorporate acknowledgment into your leadership toolbox.

Chapter 11 - Become a Coach Leader

This chapter summarizes the key concepts of coach leadership, the benefits of the coach approach to leadership and offers some tips on how to make the transition towards becoming a coach leader.

HOW THIS BOOK CAN HELP YOU

Prior to learning about Appreciative Inquiry (AI), I — like many people — focused on *solving problems*. Unfortunately, I was not aware that the unconscious mind does not process negatives. For example, if you focus on *not* eating, the unconscious mind focuses on *eating*, and so, you want to eat more. In hindsight, I can see now that the problem-solving approach produced mediocre and often superficial results. Learning AI helped me to have more productive conversations that generated solutions well beyond what the problem-solving model offered.

Prior to learning NLP and coaching, I was excellent at analyzing situations and making logical, well-informed decisions. But I did not take the time, nor did I really know how, to connect with others in a work setting. I was much younger than the people who reported to me, and I did not know how to strike the balance between learning about what was important to them and being intrusive. As a result, I erred on the side of caution and kept our interactions more formal. I don't think I was much fun to work with, and I did not do an effective job of developing others. NLP and coaching taught me how to engage at a deeper level. By being present and aware, I believe that I became a much nicer person to be around and confident enough to hand over the reins to others.

Before learning about somatics, I was on my way to becoming a robot-like leader. I relied heavily on logic, behaving the way I thought I was *supposed* to; this approach took a lot of energy. By learning to connect with my feelings and intuition, I incorporated a more compassionate approach to leadership.

By reading this book and engaging in the reflections and exercises, you will learn to:

- Initiate conversations that you previously avoided
- Ask for what you need
- Become the boss that everyone wants to work with
- Motivate, stimulate and empower others to be their best
- Enjoy more authentic relationships with yourself and others

In Closing

Many of you may already possess strong communication skills and inner awareness. If this describes you, this book will help you bring your leadership skills to the next level.

If you are ready to hit the "reset" button, this book offers you new ways of thinking about communication that will result in more authentic conversations and deeper, more satisfying relationships.

In either case, I believe this book provides the knowledge and skills that can help you become the kind of leader and person that you want to be.

Best wishes on your journey.

Barb Pierce

Note that throughout this book, I refer to the person being coached as the "coachee," regardless of whether she is your employee or a person who engages you specifically as a coach.

PART 1

THE FUNDAMENTALS

Chapter 1 - Introduction to Coaching and the CARA Process

*"The increasingly frequent 'a-ha' for most organizations it seems, is that people skills are not **soft** after all. They are absolutely hard-core business critical."*
Jane Moran

As a former military officer, I have taken many leadership courses. The books that we read were excellent, and the theories we discussed made a lot of sense. What was missing for me, however, was how to apply these leadership concepts while still being me. This is where I would have benefitted from one-on-one coaching.

At the time, there were few female military role models available to me, and I defaulted to a style of leadership that was more authoritative than suited me. Now that I am more clear about my strengths and weaknesses, I realize that I went about some things completely backwards. For example, as an introvert, I now focus on building one intimate relationship at a time rather than taking on a whole group at once. Understanding a lesson as simple as this one would have allowed me to approach my job with more confidence.

Learning the coach approach to leadership completely changed the way that I work with others. Before that, I had no idea how much easier and more fulfilling it could be to engage my coworkers as equal partners. I previously believed that I needed to maintain a safe buffer so that I did not get too close to people who were reporting to me. After all, we were not supposed to be *friends*. It took me several years to understand what it meant to connect with people who reported to me in a way that provided structure, yet allowed for people's uniqueness to surface and for a relationship to develop.

I had a wonderful experience recently where I was the project manager for the relocation of the largest building ever moved in Canada. The building was 98 years old and in poor condition — which meant plenty of possible problems. Because of the unpredictability of this type of project, and the tight timelines, the potential for stress was high; however, by cultivating strong relationships both within the team and with the other stakeholders, we were able to address issues quickly, transparently and in the spirit of partnership. When problems arose, we focused on the solutions — not on laying blame.

The result was that, not only did we complete the project on time and on budget, but that we completed it with even stronger relationships than when we began it. I believe that many working environments can provide this type of challenge and fulfillment.

THE COACH LEADER

Many people equate being a leader with actions like *making decisions, being in charge, getting others to do what the leader wants them to do* and *influencing others*. While these may be commonly understood definitions of leadership, leading in this way can be very draining. The leader must put in most of the energy, while the others follow. People in today's workplace, especially younger people, want to be included in the decision-making process and to feel like they are a vital part of an organization. They want to be treated as individuals and to contribute meaningfully.
Leaders who follow an authoritative leadership model usually end

up "telling" employees what to do and making decisions on their behalf. The authoritative leader needs to be in control and make things happen. In this model, employees are kept on a tight leash with little power to make decisions. Learning the coach approach completely changes this relationship. The coach leader does not need to know the answers — she just needs to know how to ask the right questions.

Many organizations are discovering the potential and benefits of employing the coach approach to leadership. This approach is rapidly gaining in popularity because it allows leaders to connect more deeply with people of all ages and backgrounds. Through the coach approach to leadership, leaders learn to communicate clearly in a language that resonates with the listener. More importantly, leaders learn to empower others through the artful use of setting agendas for discussions, asking powerful questions to promote learning and providing direct feedback.

What makes the coach approach unique is that it allows coach leaders to treat people both as individuals and as parts of a greater whole. Coach leaders empower and motivate each employee according to the employee's own needs. They engage others in collaborative conversations in a productive and efficient manner. These conversations are purposeful and encourage others to make choices that are in alignment with their own goals and the goals of the organization.

The coach approach allows leaders to connect more deeply with people of all ages and backgrounds.

Steve and Rob are both safety managers. When Steve does safety inspections and toolbox talks, he uses an authoritative approach. He doesn't take the time to get to know the workers as individuals. When he notices safety issues, he speaks to the workers with a forceful voice and tells them how to fix the problem. As a result, the workers avoid him and rarely ask for help with safety issues. Instead, they often ignore the safety regulations and sometimes mock Steve when he is not there. Although he does regular safety talks, the workers seem to forget or ignore his lessons, and Steve seems to be constantly complaining about their lack of compliance. He often resorts to verbal and written warnings before the problem is resolved.

When Rob does safety inspections, he always completes the inspection with one of the work supervisors present. He is friendly and calm. When safety issues arise, he asks the supervisor how he plans on dealing with them. Rob always speaks with a respectful tone and considers the supervisor to be an expert in his domain. He is skillful in asking questions to determine the supervisor's knowledge and guides him through the resolution process. As a result, no one hides safety issues from Rob. In fact, they ask his advice on how to handle them. When problems arise, Rob uses a collaborative approach to find the solution and provides advice when the supervisor does not have the expertise to address the issue at hand.

Steve creates an atmosphere of "us vs. them," while Rob creates a collaborative and trusting atmosphere. Rob does this by taking the time to get to know the workers, and by empowering the supervisor through offering assistance rather than by doing the supervisor's job for him. He treats all team members with respect.

Empowering the supervisor to come up with his own plan may initially take longer, but he will eventually learn how to make decisions on his own.

Who would you rather have as your safety manager?

WHAT IS COACHING?

Coaches use purposeful conversations to facilitate deep awareness and change. Imagine having a conversation with an employee in which you do not *tell* her what to do. Instead, you help her to understand the current situation more clearly, guide her to explore options and take actions that are in line with her and the organization's beliefs, values and vision, as well as the skills and abilities that she possesses. This takes more time up-front, but it teaches the employee how to make better decisions in the long run.

There are many styles of coaching; however, all coaching:

- Is action-oriented and future-focused with the aim of helping coachees determine and achieve personal goals
- Focuses on awakening the resourcefulness and creativity within coachees as opposed to being an advice-giving or teaching forum
- Uses questions in a skillful manner to help coachees to become more resourceful in how they deal with present and future situations
- Helps coachees to develop new capabilities, opportunities and skills
- Is a collaborative partnership between a coach and a willing

"Your gifts are not about YOU. Leadership is not about YOU. Your purpose is not about YOU. A life of significance is about SERVING those who need your gifts, your leadership, your purpose."
Kevin Hall

individual or individuals
- Connects coachees to their beliefs and values in a confidential and respectful environment
- Helps coachees to communicate in a way that allows emotions to rise without derailing the conversation

Great leaders inspire others to grow. Incorporating the coach approach to leadership allows you to help people to:

- Be more purposeful
- Be more successful
- Be happier
- Be more decisive
- Be more content
- Increase their ability to learn and grow
- Have more balance
- Have less stress, illness or self-doubt

When you employ coaching skills, your coachees will become more resourceful and insightful as a result of your work together. They will be more purposeful and will take active steps towards their desired future. Their future goals will be compelling and tangible.

Great leaders inspire others to grow.

WHAT COACHING IS NOT

Sometimes people use the words coaching, therapy, mentoring, consulting, mediating or athletic coaching interchangeably. Although there are many similarities, the processes and outcomes are quite different.

- **Therapists** have a specific certification to practice. They help identify and treat mental health issues. Coaches refer clients

" Because coaching has proven to be so effective, many major corporations invest in internal coaching and mentoring programs, usually for executives, leaders, and managers."
Marilee Goldberg

who have personal traumas to therapists. Coaches focus on the past to understand its impact on the present, with the aim of creating and achieving future-oriented goals.

- **Mentors** share knowledge and experience. Although a mentor may at times use coaching skills, a mentor is typically a more experienced person who guides and passes on her knowledge and experience to others.
- **Consultants** are hired for their skill and experience. They give specific advice and often teach their clients how to do a process or task. In the context of coaching, advice-giving may create client-coach codependency with the client looking to the coach instead of looking within for ideas.
- **Mediators** resolve disputes between two or more parties. Mediators may use coaching skills, but their focus is on facilitating conflict resolution.
- **Athletic Coaches** usually know more about the sport than the athlete. The athletic coach is responsible for both the mental and physical preparation of the athlete. The athletic coach transfers specific skills and strategies to the athlete. In life or business coaching, the coach does not instruct the coachee or give advice. The life or business coach does not normally know more about the topic than the coachee.

"Just telling people what to do, especially in stressful times, does not achieve the desired outcome of employee alignment, engagement or action. In fact, it does the direct opposite."
Jane Moran

THE CASE FOR COACHING

When leaders start seeing their employees as *coachees,* instead of as people that need to be told, directed and guided through their daily activities, they find that coachees require less direction and demonstrate more innovation and commitment.

A relationship built on the coach approach includes trust, safety, connection and confidentiality. It is a relationship where the coach guides the coachee to make her own best decisions. In a coaching conversation, the coach allows the coachee to determine her own best action steps instead of telling her what to do. The coach does this by helping the coachee explore various options and specific and tangible outcomes, all of which have been suggested and agreed to by the coachee.

Mark is a construction superintendent. Without exception, when people work with him, their feedback is very positive. The skills that make him a prized leader include the way he connects with others and his talent for providing challenges that are appropriate to the background and skill of each worker. On top of that, he is a very knowledgeable tradesman who can stay calm under difficult circumstances.

Here is how he does it.

Prior to starting work on the site, Mark interviews all of the employees to find out about their backgrounds and interests. This gives him a chance to convey his expectations and get to know them better. He believes that everyone should be treated with respect and challenged according to his or her needs.

Mark takes the time to ask questions that assess the new employee's level of knowledge and experience. At first, the new employee works with others, and Mark checks on his/her progress. The new employee is given guidance regarding the task to be completed but is not told how to do it (unless the employee asks). As much as possible, Mark assigns work that is appropriate to the knowledge and background of each worker.

The team members excel. They are visibly cheerful and enthusiastic about their work. Even the newer workers have the ability to make decisions and work independently.

Mark follows up regularly to assess progress on assigned tasks and gives clear feedback when needed. Employees know exactly where they stand with Mark. Mistakes are learned from, and carelessness is not tolerated. Mark never raises his voice.

Mark sets a strong example as a coach leader, making him a sought after construction superintendent.

THE COACH LEADER

A coach leader is someone who is engaged in a leadership role and uses the coach approach in certain circumstances. Not all circumstances are coachable and in these instances, the coach leader provides direction and guidance.

To be successful in transitioning to a coach leadership style, the coach leader must create rapport, trust and connections at a deeper level so that employees feel safe enough to engage in a new and more transparent way.

DIRECTING VS. DELEGATING

Although *directing* can appear easier in the short term, you deprive your coachees of learning how to think for themselves — especially if you don't allow them to come up with their own solutions or to make decisions. The gift of being able to make mistakes is withheld from many people today. Within predetermined boundaries, making mistakes is how people learn.

Creating and communicating an inspiring vision is a useful strategy in many situations, but this still may not allow you to connect with your employees on an individual basis. If you don't engage and negotiate with each employee, you may be setting a pace or directing a sequence of activities that is inappropriate for them.

Being a coach leader does not mean being a pushover. Sometimes employees have to do work that they don't enjoy doing. Coaching discussions may also reveal that the employee's needs and aspirations do not match their job's requirements and available growth opportunities. It is good to clarify this as well. The employee then has the opportunity to look for more suitable work (within the organization or elsewhere).

In the short term, the coach approach can take longer; however, the long-term benefits are:

- Employees do work that is in alignment with their needs and growth requirements
- Employees participate in the decision-making process, which results in improved decision-making skills
- You start developing future leaders who have had the opportunity to take responsibility for decisions within their sphere of control

---

Within predetermined boundaries, making mistakes is how people learn.

WHO USES THE COACH APPROACH?

Project managers, therapists, mentors, consultants, health care providers, parents, managers, leaders and many others use the coach approach to help them do their jobs better.

Consider how much more effective leaders would be if they had a process to uncover, empower and enlist the skills, experience and imagination of their employees, co-workers or clients.

Imagine how much loyalty and production would increase in an environment where people truly feel like valued team members.

TESTIMONIAL

"As a project manager, there are times when I simply need information or am passing on information about a project. I might be preparing a report and need to check in with one of the supervisors regarding progress or simply want to prepare new plans.

The huge benefit of the coach approach comes when problems arise. If I have built up strong relationships, the challenging discussions are much easier. When the person already knows that she is respected, feedback is accepted at face value. By asking powerful questions, she can then come up with her own solutions to the challenge."

Jen

IS THE COACH APPROACH APPROPRIATE FOR ALL SITUATIONS?

No, but it can be used more frequently than you might think.

There are times when directing, teaching and inspiring are appropriate, and there are times when a more relaxed and collaborative approach will produce greater results. The coach leader learns to discern when to employ the coach approach and when to use other leadership styles.

The bottom line for coaching is that the employee must be open to being coached by you. If the employee does not want to be coached by you, but is open to coaching, you *may* choose to find the employee another coach. This does not mean that you can't use coaching questions to get better results — it just means that you may not have the opportunity to help your employee explore and resolve issues that are affecting her performance.

"If we're growing, we're always going to be out of our comfort zone."
John C. Maxwell

Regardless of whether you have formal coaching meetings with your employees or if you use the coach approach as a process for having more productive conversations, you will find that you get more creative ideas from your employees when you ask questions that invite exploration. In addition, your employees will appreciate the opportunity to provide input on decisions that affect them.

TESTIMONIAL

"As a step-parent, I quickly realized that I would not be automatically accepted as my new teenage daughter's advisor. At first, she barely acknowledged my presence and got angry when I tried to give her advice. Looking back, I realize that I pushed too hard because I wanted to make things work smoothly.

After taking an introductory coaching course, my relationship with her improved. It's not perfect, but it is much more relaxed.

Things got better when I started watching and responding to her body language and tone of voice. I stepped back and took time to build a connection with her. I also learned to ask permission before giving advice or asking her questions. Sometimes she just wants to be heard."

Michael

How to Set Up a Coaching Conversation

When coaching conversations are used at work, the coach leader must pay special attention to how and where the meeting takes place. Sometimes coaching conversations happen spontaneously, and at other times they require preparation and planning to ensure the right conditions for success. This will be covered in more detail in Chapter 4.

You need permission to coach. If you are seeking out an employee to initiate a coaching discussion, check in to ask if it is a good time. The person may be late for a meeting or need to complete an important task.

When to Use the Coach Approach

There are times when using the coach approach is effective and times when telling or directing are more appropriate. If you pay attention to your environment, you will notice when coachable moments arise. These may occur when you are:

- Giving feedback
- Managing conflict
- Delegating
- Goal setting
- Brainstorming
- Team building

There are also times when the coach approach may not be appropriate. Examples include when you are teaching a new task or procedure, or in emergency situations.

As a leader it can be difficult to walk the fine line between leading and coaching. Each leader must find her own balance.

INTRODUCTION TO THE CARA PROCESS

Prior to codeveloping the CARA process, my coaching conversations lacked focus and were much longer than they needed to be. By learning to focus on only one topic at a time and incorporating the 4-step CARA process, my meetings became much more productive. I found that I could relax more easily into the conversation knowing that the CARA steps would provide the necessary structure for success.

The CARA process is a coaching protocol that you use during each coaching meeting. It allows you to focus on what is important — with the aim of helping your coachee identify and break old patterns and develop new behaviors. Each meeting results in an action plan and a summary of the key lessons learned.

The CARA process was developed to help you guide coachees through the identification, exploration, resolution and follow-through of a topic in a time-efficient manner. By following the CARA process, coaches greatly improve their rate of success in helping others achieve tangible and meaningful results.

The CARA process also works extremely well with laser coaching, which are 10- to 20- minute results-oriented meetings that allow the coach to guide the coachee to quickly identify and resolve key issues. As a coach leader, you will likely engage in multiple short, casual coaching meetings as situations arise rather than weekly 30-60 minute pre-planned coaching meetings. As your skills improve, the CARA process allows you to guide your coachee through the analysis and resolution of a topic in 4-10 minutes.

The CARA process employs four steps:

- **Connection**: This step involves creating a safe environment, rapport and a meaningful connection with the coachee. It is important to take the time you need to connect with your coachee — if she does not trust you she may not be able to move towards resolving her issue at anything deeper than a superficial level.

- **Awareness**: This step involves helping the coachee to experience her topic clearly and objectively. It is important to take the time to ensure that the coachee is working on the most important topic at hand, or you will achieve only mediocre or superficial results.
- **Resources**: This step involves helping the coachee to investigate new possibilities of action and to increase her resourcefulness.
- **Action**: This step involves turning the results of the resources exploration into action steps with clear and measurable outcomes. It also includes a summary of the key learning points (takeaways).

The CARA process is not linear. You can move freely between the steps to meet your coachee's needs in the best way possible.

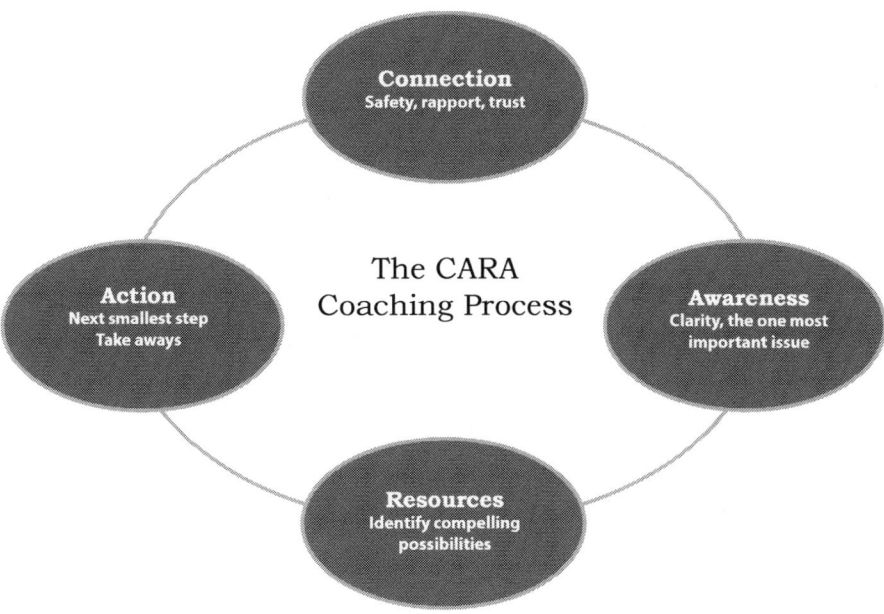

Alison is a project manager. Prior to her coach training, projects were mentally draining and occupied many of her waking hours. She tended to carry decisions on her own shoulders and did not always share information that others required. This approach affected the quality of her sleep, her energy and her enjoyment of these projects. She was very good at organizing, but wanted to learn to relax and go with the flow more easily.

By employing the coach approach, she became the hub for information storage and dissemination, and also began sharing information she was acquiring on the job. She began empowering others to make and implement decisions and helped to foster a more relaxed, yet focused, work environment. When problems arose on projects, she engaged in difficult conversations as soon as possible to clear the air before there was too much water under the bridge.

Instead of *telling* subordinates what do to, she learned to ask powerful questions to develop the subordinate's leadership skills. If a deadline was in jeopardy, rather than jumping into problem-solving mode, she asked questions like:

> "What are the options to get back on track?"
> "What is most important?"
> "What do you recommend?"

This approach allowed her supervisors to grow, take calculated risks and increase their self-confidence. Her reputation changed from that of someone who is somewhat difficult to work with to that of someone who is respected and appreciated as a leader.

WHAT TO EXPECT

Try not to have too many expectations about how coaching conversations will unfold. Very often, the topic that the coachee wants to focus on is merely a safe way for her to introduce the underlying topic.

When you read the sample coaching conversations at the end of each chapter, you will notice that the discussions are very personal and intimate. This intimacy cannot, and should not, be forced; however, once present, the coachee has the freedom to explore and be honest with herself.

Whether you are working with a CEO, a receptionist, a parent, or a student, coaching rarely focuses entirely on mechanical elements such as preparing a business plan or a to-do list. More often, the coaching is about identifying underlying behavior patterns and ways of thinking that are preventing the achievement of the goal. In summary, be prepared to be surprised, and don't force the conversation to go in a direction that you believe is more appropriate.

All of the conversations in this book are real conversations that took place between a coach and coachee. The conversations are shared with permission; however, names and other identifying details have been altered to maintain confidentiality.

You will notice that the coach speaks for only a small portion of each discussion. Coaches aim to ask questions using 5-7 words (or less). In addition, the coach aims to create a pace that is calming and provides plenty of opportunities for self-reflection.

REFLECTION

When could you benefit from employing the coach approach instead of directing/telling?

EXERCISE

Over the next week, on at least one occasion, resist the urge to tell your employee what to do or how to do it. Instead, ask questions to help him or her discover the answer to the question or issue at hand.

❝❝ A COACHING CONVERSATION

The following is a typical coaching conversation. Notice how the coach navigates between the four steps of the CARA process. During the actual conversation, the coach gradually slowed her speech to model calmness.

Coach: I want to assure you that you will have full confidentiality. We have 10 minutes together. What would you like to focus on?

Coachee: I want to shut my brain off at night so I can sleep. (**Topic**)

Coach: What is happening now?

Coachee: I have trouble getting to sleep. My mind is too active.

Coach: How would you sleep if you could shut your brain off?

Coachee - Better, more rested, more even, more effective.

Coach: How would you feel, with a restful sleep?

Coachee: I'd feel peaceful, grounded, present.

Coach: How do you feel now after you sleep?

Coachee: Tired, foggy, lethargic.

Coach: How is this affecting your life right now?

Coachee: I am exhausted. I need more sleep.

Coach: We have 8 minutes left, what specifically would you like to achieve at the end of our meeting?

Coachee: I would like a strategy to get to sleep at night, so my mind will not be jumping from one thing to the next. To slow things down. (**Outcome**)

Coach: Do you want to focus on the strategy or on letting go of whatever is keeping your brain active?

Coachee: The strategy. There will always be something that my brain can focus on. I need to know how to turn it off.

Coach: Turn it off?

Coachee: When I lie down to sleep. I want my brain to slow down so I fall asleep easily.

Coach: At the end of our meeting, how will you know that you have solved this?

Coachee: I will know what to do when my mind starts jumping around.

(Clarifying the outcome)

Coach: What will you feel in your body when you can slow your brain down and know how to fall asleep?

Coachee: Calm, relaxed, slow.

Coach: Where will you feel that?

Coachee: Everywhere. Slow, relaxed, calm (Note that she is already speaking slower and calmer, and that the coach speaks slower and calmer.)

Coach: When you picture or imagine this, what comes up?

Coachee: (pause) I think that I am doing too much stuff before I go to bed. My system is revved up. I need to calm down before going to bed.

Coach: What would that be like?

Coachee: 30 minutes before bed, I would stop doing chores. I would sit and read. Maybe even meditate. When I prepare for bed, I would not rush things like brushing my teeth.

Coach: How will that feel?

Coachee: Calm and peaceful. I will start slowing down for sleeping.

Coach: What else do you notice?

Coachee: The more I feel the need to rush, the more I need to slow down. Rushing to get to sleep has the opposite effect.

Coach: What is it that you will be creating instead of the rushing?

Coachee: Calmness.

Coach: How are you feeling now about sleep? **(Check-in against the desired outcome)**

Coachee: Great. I will start winding down, slowing down at least 30 minutes before sleeping. I will slow down my movements, sit quietly, do things calmly.

Coach: (big, slow breath) Is there anything else that you will do?

Coachee: (big, slow breath) Sleep is important. I will set aside the time that I need to prepare for it.

Coach: What are you taking away from today's meeting? **(Summary of the key lessons learned)**

Coachee: I need to slow down and start winding down at least 30 minutes before sleeping.

Coach: Thank you.

SUMMARY

- The coach approach allows you to engage others in collaborative conversations.
- Coaches use purposeful conversations to facilitate deep awareness and change.
- When you employ coaching conversations, your coachees will become more resourceful and insightful.
- A coach leader is someone who is engaged in a leadership role and uses the coach approach in certain circumstances.
- Coaching conversations require safety.
- The coach must receive permission from the coachee to ask coaching questions.
- The CARA process includes 4-steps:
  - Connection
  - Awareness
  - Resources
  - Action
- The coach can cycle back and forth between the steps to achieve the desired results from the conversation.

Chapter 2 - Appreciative Inquiry

Learning about appreciative inquiry (AI) sparked an "aha" moment that forever changed how I interact with others. The concepts fit in perfectly with NLP principles and my understanding of the way the unconscious mind works. I started implementing AI right away with excellent results. I found that approaching conversations through the lens of AI created a more optimistic tone for these conversations and moved the discussion from a focus on what was *wrong* to *what was possible*; this helped my coachees get to a place of understanding and possibility much more quickly.

Like many people, I used to focus on *solving the problem* during coaching discussions. I now know that focusing on the problem brings even more attention to the problem rather than to the solution. For example, when you are biking on a trail, the more you focus on the big rock that you want to avoid, the more likely you are to hit it. To successfully navigate the obstacle, you instead look beyond the rock to the place where you want your wheels to go. The same thing happens with work or personal problems. The more you focus on the thing you don't want, the more of it you're going to get.

As a leader, you will find that incorporating AI changes the way you connect with others. It pulls the other person out of a problem state, gives you tools to encourage others to think for themselves and removes you from the role of solving other people's problems.

APPRECIATIVE INQUIRY

With AI, you not only provide feedback on what is working well, but also actively cultivate behaviors that will benefit the other person and the organization. The process involves dialogue and the creation of a partnership so that the recipient actively participates in the process to determine what to focus on and how to move forward at a manageable pace.

Developed by David Cooperrider, Ph.D., of Case Western Reserve University, AI is an approach to change that focuses on what is working well and how to build on successes rather than on problem identification and solving. It can be used one-on-one or in large groups and is appropriate for personal change work, strategic planning, organization redesign and evaluations.

Although society has historically been in favor of problem-solving approaches to generate change, there has been significant research in the past fifty years regarding the benefits of positive thinking. Simply put: you get more of what you choose to focus on.

In AI, you see your coachees as resourceful and capable, and you encourage those attributes. Asking your coachees to focus on positive stories with the intent of learning what worked in the past encourages even more of this behavior. In solution-focused brief therapy, a technique on which AI is based, "the aim is to start the solution process rather than to stop the complaint pattern"[1]

With AI, you can do a whole lot more than just solve the problem.

APPRECIATIVE COACHING

Appreciative coaches guide their coachees toward the future, while accessing and building upon the best of their past. The advantage of an AI-based approach when coaching is that the questions lead the coachee to experience a positive frame of mind. It is from this place/state that the coachee is able to develop new possibilities.

The language used by both the coach and the coachee has an impact on the coachee's reality and potential for future changes. When the coachee is in an unresourceful frame of mind, she often can't see the possibilities available to her. When this occurs, the simple act of changing physiology through different postures, storytelling or visualizations allows the coachee to see her situation more favorably and opens her up to more possibilities.

AI is not like problem solving where you look for what is wrong and try to fix it. Instead, you focus on the positive, but in a way that promotes learning and discovery. The AI process is not a sugar-coated pep talk, but a true inquiry into best practices in which the coach listens for words, phrases and metaphors that tell the coach what is important to the coachee.

---

1   Whitney, D., & Trosten-Bloom, A. (200). The power of appreciative inquiry: A practical guide to positive change.   (2nd ed.). San Francisco, CA: Berrett-Koehler Publishers.

Although the AI process does not encourage negative stories, when one comes up, the facilitator/coach uses these stories to generate ideas about what was missing, so that learning can still take place. If the negative stories are suppressed or ignored, then there may be resentment, and the coachee may feel that the process is biased or ineffective.

> When we are in an unresourceful frame of mind, we often can't see the possibilities available to us.

Appreciative Inquiry	Problem Solving
Focus on what you want	Focus on what went wrong
Lessons from the past	Blame
Positive frame of mind	Fear of making mistakes
Anticipation	Judging
Suggestions	Complaints

66 A COACHING DISCUSSION

Notice how the coach uses the coachee's language without interpreting or altering it, and encourages the coachee to focus on what he *wants*, not what he does *not* want.

"We don't see things the way they are. We see things the way WE are."
The Talmud

Coach: What would you like to focus on?
Coachee: My teachers hate me. I hate school. I always get in trouble even when I am trying not to.
Coach: Sounds like it's not much fun being there.
Coachee: Yup.
Coach: What would you like to be different?
Coachee: I guess for it not to suck.
Coach: What things do you like to do?
Coachee: Skateboard, BMX, videogames.
Coach: What is it like when you do those things?
Coachee: Fun. I am with my friends, chilling, there's no pressure.
Coach: Fun, friends, no pressure, chilling.
Coachee: Yeah.
Coach: What is the opposite of sucking?
Coachee: Awesome.
Coach: Awesome. (Pause) Is there anything about school that is awesome? Friends? No pressure?
Coachee: Gym, recess...art.
Coach: What is different about those classes?
Coachee: The teachers are not so uptight.
*Coach: How are **you** different in those classes?*
Coachee: There is no pressure in those classes. I can just have fun.
Coach: How would you like to get along with your teachers?
Coachee: More relaxed, less pressure.
....
(The coachee is now in a frame of mind that is more receptive to a productive discussion.) 99

THE FIVE PRINCIPLES OF APPRECIATIVE INQUIRY*

1. The Constructionist Principle

A person's future is based on what she already knows and can build upon. To accomplish this, the coach helps the client recall a time, in any context, when the client had what she is seeking.

CASE STUDY

George was recently promoted based on his ability to manage effectively in a fast-paced production environment. He was concerned because his new job required him to manage engineering, as well as production, and he was not connecting with the engineering team. He felt that the engineering team did not respect him. The team was hostile and did not share key information with him. He had started looking for employment elsewhere, but was willing to try coaching to change his current situation.

Employing the constructionist principle, the topic for inquiry was elicited. George chose to focus on "creating a trusting and respectful team." The coach then helped him to recall a team experience in which there was trust and respect. George said that in his former experiences, the manager took the time to clarify roles, personal responsibilities and the future vision of the team. The manager also connected with and learned about each individual. George had just assumed that he would be treated with respect, but had not taken active steps to cultivate it.

Instead of looking for new work, George focused on connecting with the team leaders, clarifying roles and responsibilities and setting team goals.

2. The Positive Principle

Seeing the past and future in positive terms creates a strong resource anchor, which builds confidence and resourcefulness. If the coachee focuses on the negative, the coach's job is to get her to focus on the lessons she learned from that experience or on what the coachee *wants*, rather than what she does *not* want (because a person amplifies what she pays attention to). [2]

CASE STUDY

Mary was promoted from project coordinator to project manager. Project coordinators typically report through a project manager. Project managers have responsibility and accountability for the entire project.

The technical lead of the project, who used to be quite friendly when Mary was the project coordinator, started being rude to her and seemed to enjoy "telling her what to do." Mary was finding this frustrating and did not feel that the technical lead respected her skill set and what she offered the project.

When Mary was asked what she wanted to focus on during the appreciative coaching meeting, she immediately complained about what was wrong with her current situation and said that she was tired of being disrespected by the technical lead. To change her frame of mind, she was then asked to state what she *wanted*, rather than what she did *not* want.

Mary then framed her topic in positive terms: "I want to create a respectful relationship with my technical lead where we are both

2   Orem, S. L., Binkert, J., & Clancy, A. L. (2007). Appreciative coaching: A positive process for change. (p. 121). San Francisco, CA: John Wiley & Sons, Inc.

clear on our roles and how we support each other. Ultimately, I am responsible for the project and he reports to me, not the other way around." The meeting then focused on creating the positive conditions that she wanted, rather than on "solving the problem."

3. The Simultaneity Principle

The future happens in — and as a result of — the present. This means that the way we ask questions leads the client to focus on the problem or the solution.

CASE STUDY

Mark was successful in sales. He connected naturally with his clients and always exceeded his targets. After he was transferred to marketing, he stopped enjoying his work. He found the paperwork boring, and did not like preparing plans and doing market research. He was thinking of asking for a transfer back to sales, even though this would limit his long-term growth in the company.

When describing his problem, he launched into a rant about how he was never going to progress in his career, and that he did not know where to begin with the market research.

To reframe the topic, the coach asked, "Mark, I understand what you *don't* want. What *do* you want?" Mark then said that he wanted to keep his career options open and learn to excel at marketing.

The coach asked him if he had ever had an experience of learning a new sales skill and eventually excelling at it, then related that experience to excelling at marketing.

4. The Poetic Principle

The coach helps the coachee rewrite her life stories to better fit how she sees herself. This allows life stories to be reframed to create a new and more positive future.

CASE STUDY

Marie had found new employment after leaving a difficult work situation. She felt that her former boss was harassing her, but she did not feel comfortable making a complaint. Instead, she decided to find a new job.

In her new job, Marie felt that she was being asked to do tasks that were not part of her job's responsibilities, but she was afraid to stand up for herself. At first it was small things, but the requests were getting bigger, and she was starting to get angry. Once again, she was wondering if she needed to look for another job.

Although the former job was not a positive experience, her coach helped Marie grow by exploring how and when she could have established boundaries, and how to apply those lessons to her current job.

5. The Anticipatory Principle

The coach helps the coachee to experience her desired future. This helps to shape current behaviors that will ultimately lead towards that future.

CASE STUDY

Alex wanted to become the CEO of his company by the time he was 50. At the time of coaching, he was the VP of operations and had previous experience in sales, marketing and customer service. Although his background was well-rounded, he did not have expertise in accounting. He knew that a CEO must have a strong understanding of accounting to be successful but did not know how to acquire this knowledge base.

The coach helped Alex create a "vision" of his future. When he experienced this future vision, the coach helped him to understand who he was and what skills he had in order to be successful. The coach then co-created a long-term plan with Alex that helped him to build the skills and experience necessary to achieve his goal.

* Information about the principles and the 4-D cycle was extracted primarily from two sources: *The Power of Appreciative Inquiry – a Practical Guide to Positive Change,* by Diana Whitney and Amanda Trosten-Bloom, and *Appreciative Coaching – A Positive Process for Change*, by Sara Orem, Jacqueline Binkert and Ann L. Clancy.

Ms. Orem, Binkert and Clancy's approach to coaching incorporates positive psychology, positive organizational scholarship and solution focused brief therapy. They have conducted independent research to develop their appreciative coaching model.

THE 4-D CYCLE

The AI model is straightforward and has four simple steps that can be linked to the CARA model:

- Discovery
- Dream
- Design
- Destiny

Incorporating the 4-D cycle into your leadership approach will help take the drama out of your conversations and turn problem solving into solution finding.

I noticed an immediate change in the energy of my coaching conversations when I started using the AI model. By acknowledging how my coachee was feeling at the beginning of the conversation and how the situation was affecting her life, she felt heard and ready to explore new possibilities. Once the problem was on the table and acknowledged, she was free to focus on finding a solution. I noticed that, without prompting, the coachees soon started using language that focused on the solution instead of the problem, and that the resources step flowed more easily.

By providing a structure through which to reframe the situation, the AI process helps to put participants in a more resourceful state of mind in which they are able to focus on finding the solution rather than on complaining or blaming others. It puts the participants in a position to create change rather than be victims of their circumstances.

1. Discovery: "The Best of What Is"
The discovery step is about creating a connection, finding out what is important to the coachee, and developing a positive resource state in the coachee. In this stage, the coachee generates

positive images related to the topic being discussed with the aim of creating a more open outlook about the topic. For example, if the coachee is focusing on building a stronger team, you can say:

- "Think back to your most positive team experience."
- "Describe a peak experience when working with a team."
- "What do you want more of when working with your team?"

The coachee is invited to share a story that describes a positive team experience. This generates a resourceful feeling and builds confidence based on remembering what led to past successes. The coach asks probing questions to deepen the experience and generate lessons from the story. Questions are based on "what worked" rather than "what was wrong."

These personal stories generate emotions and feelings that touch the coachee at a deep level and can lead to significant transformations.

This step is similar to the connection and awareness steps in the CARA model.

2. Dream: "What Might Be?"

A future vision is developed by the coachee based on the themes uncovered during the discovery phase. The vision, which incorporates the coachee's values and past accomplishments, is described in positive language (i.e. what you *want*, not what you *don't* want). The coachee then has the opportunity to explore the desired outcome and bring it to life as a compelling possibility.

The dream serves to create an unconscious connection that leads the coachee towards that outcome. It is similar to the way athletes rehearse their athletic event in advance. This technique is proven to lead towards more positive and successful outcomes.

If your coachee is having difficulty with this step, you can ask:

- "Allow yourself to float out to _____(time in the future), what do you notice?"
- "If anything were possible...what would you want?"
- "If you could have three wishes, what would they be?"

This step is similar to the resources step in the CARA model.

3. Design: "What Should Be"

In this step, the coach helps the coachee to bring the dream into focus. A bold statement of what the coachee wants to happen is developed. It presents an image of how things will be when the new ideas are incorporated.

In the design step, short and long-term goals are developed.

This step is similar to the action step in the CARA model.

4. Destiny: "Create What Will Be"

Specific tasks are identified to help achieve these goals, and possibilities are identified and implemented. Destiny activities can include the development of new policies, processes, evaluation systems and structures. This step includes monitoring and soliciting feedback. It is a time to celebrate accomplishments. It can also be a time to conclude the relationship, or design bigger or different goals by starting the AI process over again.

This step equates to the follow-up coaching meetings throughout the coaching relationship in which the coachee works on accomplishing her coaching plan.

EXERCISE

Facilitate an appreciative inquiry discussion at work or at home.

Guidelines

1. Find an individual or group who would like to make a change (a better work environment, a more trusting team, more on-time deliveries, etc.) and is willing to engage in the AI process.
2. Facilitate a discussion using the appreciative inquiry approach to create a sustainable change. It could be one discussion or a series of discussions.
3. Summarize:
    *   The topic
    *   Your approach
    *   What worked
    *   What did not work
    *   What you will do differently next time
    *   Your successes and lessons learned

"Every thought we think is creating our future."
Louise Hay

REFLECTION

How can you incorporate appreciative inquiry into your work or life?

❝❝ A COACHING CONVERSATION

Notice how the coach helps the coachee focus on what the coachee *wants*, not what she does *not* want.

"To accomplish great things, we must not only act, but also dream; not only plan, but also believe."
Anatole France

Coach: What would you like to focus on today?

Coachee: I am thinking of pursuing a different career, maybe even going back to school, but I am facing financial pressure at home.

Coach: What would be most valuable to focus on today?

Coachee: To find out if career coaching is something I want to do for the rest of my life.

Coach: What would you have at the end of the conversation that you don't have now?

Coachee: To understand if it is something I would do regardless of the money.

Coach: What would you like to explore?

Coachee: I want to talk with as many people as I can in the career coaching field to learn their experiences, things I can't learn in books. I want to be completely open and not have assumptions. Even this morning, I was conscious of finding my own state of being, finding my own way, my own path.

Coach: Is that the bigger subject? Finding your own being?

Coachee: Yes.

Coach: What would that be like?

Coachee: There are a lot of people that don't have the chance to talk to someone. It is not about the job; it is about how can you contribute and make a difference.

Coach: As you are helping people, what is that doing for you?

Coachee: It feels great, I love to listen and I like to use the skill set I have to show them a different perspective.

Coach: What is that like?

Coachee: Peace, joy, the smile, I am grateful that they shared.

Coach: When you are feeling that, where do you feel it in your body?

Coachee: I feel light. Why not do it more?

Coach: That is a good question. As you hear yourself say that, what comes to you?

Coachee: Fear. I already have a job. Will I be able to let that go? That is my biggest fear.

Coach: Would you say it is the fear that is stopping you from the 'beingness' that you talked about?

Coachee: The fear of being judged, too. My friends think I have it so good. I have a permanent job. I am supporting my wife and in-laws. They live with us.

Coach: We have a few minutes remaining, what would give you the biggest value: to explore career coaching, the state of being, or the fear?

Coachee: Explore the career coaching.

Coach: When you say explore career coaching, what would you like to get out of the conversation?

Coachee: To know if coaching is right for me.

Coach: What would you like to walk away with?

Coachee: To learn more about coaching, develop tools to not have the fear anymore.

Coach: What will you have instead of fear?

Coachee: Confidence.

Coach: What comes first, confidence or to know if coaching is right for you?

Coachee: Knowing about coaching brings confidence.

Coach: From what you know about coaching, what is your vision of being a coach?

Coachee: The end goal is to bring awareness to people. To help them find joy in their careers.

Coach: Picture that you've already done it. How does that feel?

Coachee: It feels amazing. I would be smiling more. My journey is to do that. I would be fully satisfied, no regrets.

Coach: What is your next smallest step?

Coachee: Talk to more career coaches, learn from them. Get more ideas, take notes, see how to promote coaching to a wider audience. You have to reach people.

Coach: Do you have the understanding you wanted from this conversation?

Coachee: Yes. I don't have my answer, but I know my next steps to get there.

Coach: Your next smallest step is to talk to as many people as you can. When will you do that?

Coachee: I would like to talk to you. Next week I am meeting with a coach from the career centre to learn what they are doing. I am interviewing a career counselor to learn the difference between career coaching, counseling and consulting.

Coach: How's your confidence?

Coachee: I don't have all of the answers, but I am approaching the exploration from a place of confidence instead of fear.

Coach: How will you hold yourself accountable for your actions?

Coachee: I will have these conversations in the next two weeks.

Coach: What are you taking away from our conversation?

Coachee: You made me realize that it feels good to help others. Second, I need to talk to different coaches let go of the fear.

"

SUMMARY

- Appreciative Inquiry (AI) focuses on what you want, rather than what is wrong.
- The five principles of AI are:
    - The Constructionist Principle
    - The Positive Principle
    - The Simultaneity Principle
    - The Poetic Principle
    - The Anticipatory Principle
- The AI model incorporates four steps:
    - Discovery
    - Dream
    - Design
    - Destiny

Chapter 3 - Somatic Coaching

"Our bodies are brilliant. They act as compasses, letting us know when we're headed in the right direction and when we're not."
Dr. Lissa Rankin

Many people are uncomfortable lowering their defensive walls in the workplace and instead act in a formal and "businesslike" manner. While this approach seems sensible and safe, it can lead to superficial working relationships and mediocre results. This approach does not promote loyalty and long-term relationships.

The supervisors that I have most valued in my career were people who were friendly, genuine and sincerely interested in my well-being. I liked feeling that these people truly cared about me, and not just my output. I enjoyed my interactions with them; I didn't just survive them.

Today, I still appreciate working with people who respect and take the time to get to know me, not just my skills. I don't necessarily want to be *friends* with my supervisor and co-workers, but I do want to feel that we can have a friendly relationship.

SOMATIC AWARENESS AS A LEADERSHIP SKILL

People today are often rewarded for making decisions based on logic. While this approach is useful, you will make even better decisions when you also pay attention to your intuition.

Successful leaders know who they are and what is important to them. They have the "know-how" to tap into their intuition about themselves, other people and situations. These leaders have developed the skills to move beyond intellectual analysis. They not only know how to listen to their internal signals, but they also have the courage to follow them, even when the resulting decisions or changes in thinking don't follow logic.

Unfortunately, many people either do not know how to listen to their body or they habitually ignore the signals as a safety measure because they are unable or unwilling to deal with their emotions. This chapter will remind you how to connect internally, how to notice and identify feelings, emotions and energy, and how to translate that information into action.

> Noticing and acting on your "gut feeling" or instincts will help you make decisions that are in alignment with all of who you are.

COACH THE WHOLE PERSON

Coaching rarely focuses entirely on routine tasks like developing action plans, goal setting or writing business plans. Often the coachee has sought coaching because something is not working in her life or because she may want something different. Obstacles can include personal challenges such as:

- "My 15-year-old son started using drugs, and I can't focus on my job."
- "Our teams need to work together, but I despise the other manager. At meetings he is constantly trying to make me look bad."
- "I have finally achieved the position I have been coveting for the past five years, and now I just feel disappointed. I am bored, and I wonder if I will ever feel happy."

"Trust yourself. You know more than you think you do."
Benjamin Spock

In order to coach the whole person, you need to speak with the body, mind and soul of your coachees. Too often, coaches only talk with the mind. This results in follow-up action steps being decided upon at the intellectual level, which requires a heavy reliance on willpower, lists and detailed action plans to make changes. When you coach at this level, the discussions can be superficial and changes take an enormous amount of energy to implement and maintain.

When you also coach the body and soul, the discussions become more intimate and the resulting changes flow more naturally. The coachee often does not need to *do* anything to make the changes happen. Rather, she simply needs to *be* the change.

INTUITION

Whether you choose to pay attention or not, you have access to instincts and intuition to help guide your decisions and actions. Unfortunately, many people are either unaware of these feelings or choose to ignore the signals in favor of logic.

Intuition is when the hairs rise on the back of your neck when you feel unsafe, when you feel a stab of fear in your chest, when your gut feels uneasy or, conversely, when you have a "good feeling" about someone. Intuition is also the thoughts that pop into your head that provide insights beyond any words that were spoken. It helps you understand the themes that operate beneath the words. Intuition helps you notice when other people's emotions or body language are not congruent with the message they are delivering.

Intuition helps you understand what is operating beneath the surface.

These feelings and flashes of awareness are provided by your unconscious mind, which is not only the storehouse of all of your memories, but is also responsible for involuntary responses such as breathing, pumping blood and other basic physiological functions and primal reactions to potential threats (instincts).

By learning to listen to and act upon your instincts, you will make better decisions that account for factors that your conscious mind has no awareness of.

TESTIMONIAL

"Recently, the yoga business that I was working for was shut down because of building permit problems. When I first heard that it was being shut down, I was told that we may need to deliver the classes elsewhere. No matter what anyone else says, I am going to check in with my body about how I feel about decisions. The first thing I did was stop, go inside and determine what the best course of action would be for me in that moment. By checking in with what was best for me, the result was also best for everyone. I did not try to fake it or perform. I believe that making authentic decisions is usually the right decision overall for the larger circle."

Sandy

WHAT IS SOMATIC COACHING?

In somatic coaching, coaches listen to their intuition, feelings and emotions and also pay attention to those of the coachee. According to Kay and Mcculloch, "(t)he process brings about change by working 'through the body' to awaken senses and feelings, bringing us more alive, present and open to possibility."[3]

Your intuition helps you to hear beyond the spoken words. As a coach, you provide a tremendous service in helping your coachee get in touch with her intuition, feelings and emotions — especially when the coachee is blind to her underlying feelings.

Learn how to listen to and act on your instincts.

The body never lies. Even if your conscious mind overlays logic onto your intuitive messages, your body will continue to react to its circumstances. For example, if you are in an unsafe situation, your body may warn you of danger via the hairs standing up on your neck. If you convince yourself the well-dressed and smooth-talking person in front of you is honest and trustworthy, your body will continue to make you feel uneasy about him.

Sometimes following your intuition seems to be more trouble than it's worth, but in the long run, it will steer you in the right direction. Learn to trust your instincts. They will keep you safe.

---

3   Kay, R., & McCulloch, R. (May 2007). Building Capacity for Change: The Power of the Body. AI Practitioner, 34.

HOW SOMATIC COACHING WORKS

Somatics is the study of the body; this is not new. Yogis, martial artists, t'ai chi practitioners and many others have explored and passed down knowledge about the body for thousands of years. When incorporating somatics into the coaching process, the coach helps the coachee to connect with her body sensations, emotions and insights provided by the unconscious mind. This helps the coachee to be more self-aware and to notice when things shift inside.

Somatic Awareness	Analysis and Logic
• Feel and identify emotions • Recognize and interpret "gut reactions" or intuition • Be present to emotions, without needing to cover them or change them to something "better" or different • Read own and other people's body language	• Analyze data • Review pros and cons • Think ahead to the next steps • Look to the past for answers

WORKING WITH THE BODY

Yogis refer to five layers that lead towards discovery of the self. From outermost to innermost, the layers are:

Physical

The physical layer — your body — also includes what you "consume" (your five senses, food, environment, etc.). You become aware of this layer through mindful physical movement, while noticing areas of strength, tightness, looseness, openness, etc. Paying attention to this layer brings greater body awareness.

Energy

Energy is also known as prana or chi. It is the vital energy, or life force, that exists in all of us and flows through meridians (energy pathways) and chakras (energy centers). When trained, you can perceive this life force and notice both blockages and the flow of energy. In addition to becoming aware of your subtle energy, you can also influence it through breathing techniques, mindfulness, the way you think and physical activities.

Mental/Emotional (The Mind)

The mental/emotional layer is known as your conscious mind; it allows you to process information and remember it. You gain information through your five senses, which is then processed through filters that were created as a result of your life experiences. You become aware of this layer through self-awareness and the practice of viewing a situation from an objective perspective.

Wisdom/Intuition

The wisdom/intuition layer is the place of *knowing* and allows you to experience the objective truth. This layer is also known as the unconscious mind. You learn about this layer through mindfulness practices and through paying attention to your intuition.

Bliss (Your Authentic Self)

Bliss is the place of peace, joy and being yourself.

Learning to listen to your intuition will lead you towards becoming yourself and to the place of bliss. To get to your bliss — your authentic self — you must identify and pass through your physical, energetic and mental layers, and get to the "heart of the matter." This is the place where you can reside in peace and joy — where you can simply be yourself.

Once you realize that you already *know* but simply need to learn how to listen to that voice, you start making decisions and acting in ways that honor who you are. When changes are accompanied by emotional insights, or shifts, that anchor the positive resource states, the desired outcome is more likely to "feel" right and be easier to implement. Even people who have been successful by relying on logical thinking will benefit tremendously from connecting with their bodies, emotions and energy.

HOW TO CATALYZE CHANGE USING SOMATIC COACHING

Self-awareness is the key to catalyzing change and growth. This awareness typically begins at the outermost layer and moves inwards; however, the process is not always linear. The most powerful changes often originate at the innermost layers.

Change at the Body Layer

Basic needs must be met to create the conditions that allow for deeper focus and inner awareness. You need to have an adequate supply of food, sleep, clean air and a safe physical environment. Additionally, being in good physical health can provide a foundation that allows for deep reflection and physical stamina from which to look inward.

It is common knowledge that athletes use creative visualizations to improve performance and learn new skills. The athletes rehearse these new movements and sequences (through visualizations) over and over to integrate new patterns. Such techniques can also be used to catalyze personal growth and inner awareness. To accomplish this, coaches help coachees determine what changes they want to make, then preview how they will be in the future with the new skills and techniques that they are working on. This in turn creates new neural connections that help to engage and maintain the process of change.

During a coaching meeting, Jim, an independent HR consultant, wanted to focus on creating more business. As the conversation unfolded, he kept mentioning that he had been taken advantage of by the company he was on contract with for the past 10 years. Despite feeling resentful and angry, he was unable to make a clean break from this company even though the financial return was negligible.

Prior to exploring new possibilities, it was important for Jim to address any feelings of resentment and being taken advantage of so that he would not transpose these feelings onto any new contracts or partnerships. Jim decided that, in the future, he needed to be clear in his requests and be more assertive. He also wanted to create mutually respectful relationships.

When asked what it would be like to be clear in his message, assertive and willing to walk away from relationships that are not mutually respectful, Jim said he would be strong, confident and satisfied. We discussed times in his past when he felt those positive feelings, and then transposed those lessons to his current situation.

Based on his insights, Jim realized that he was successful in the past when he put energy into the tasks up-front and completed them quickly and boldly. This in turn generated confidence, satisfaction and energy.

His next step was to increase his exercise regimen to remember the feeling of boldly taking action and experiencing the energizing results. At the next meeting, he was then able to explore how to be more assertive and clear with his requests without dwelling on the fear of being taken advantage of.

Change at the Energetic Layer

Once you know your "baseline" of energy flow, feelings and emotions, you know when things have changed. For example, you have probably heard people say, "something feels wrong, but I just can't put my finger on it." By learning how to become centered and focused inward on your body and your internal energy, you differentiate between the many emotions and feelings that you experience, and the flow of energy within your body.

Change at the Mental/Emotional Layer

Change at the mental/emotional layer requires that you become familiar with the personal beliefs, values and perceptions that guide how you interpret events. You learn to become an objective observer rather than to interpret your situation based on the filter of your past experiences.

Change at the Intuitive Layer

Change is not required at this layer. You simply learn to pay attention to the intuitive layer, which allows you to become more certain of who you really are. You notice when your body reacts to certain situations and you pay attention to your "gut feeling" when making decisions.

The Bliss Layer

When you are fully present to all moments and act in ways that are in alignment with your authentic self, you will be at peace, regardless of the situation you face. Your goal is to assist your coachee in uncovering and becoming her true self.

In somatic coaching, you help your coachee move beyond her intellect to become aware of her body, emotions and energy. You help her understand where and how her body is impacted by her thoughts, feelings, emotions and energy.

SOMATIC COACHING

You can assess somatic competence in your coachee by asking her what she is feeling in her body during the coaching meeting. [4] If your coachee is not self-aware, she may benefit from a centering exercise. You can encourage her to notice her body (tightness, openness), energy flow and general state of health.

When you become more aware of your body, you notice more quickly the impact that different people and situations have on you. At first, you might notice only significant feelings and emotions. As you become more skilled, you notice more subtle feelings and emotions. This eventually allows you to make changes before these feelings become overwhelming.

QUESTIONS THAT PROMOTE SOMATIC AWARENESS

Body Layer

- Where do you feel that?
- What are you feeling?
- What does that feel like?

Energetic Layer

- Where do you feel that energy?
- Is there an energy blockage?
- What are you noticing about your energy?

"I tell you, deep inside you is a fountain of bliss, a fountain of joy. Deep inside your center core is truth, light, love, there is no guilt there, there is no fear there. Psychologists have never looked deep enough."

Sri Sri Ravi Shankar

---

4   (2008). C. Wahl, C. Scriber & B. Bloomfield (Eds.), On becoming a leadership coach: A holistic approach to coaching excellence (1st ed., p. 102). New York, NY: Palgrave Macmillan

Mental/Emotional Layer

- What emotion is coming up?
- If you could experience that objectively, what would you notice?

Intuitive Layer

- What is your "gut feeling" about that?
- What does your intuition tell you?
- If anything were possible, what would you tell yourself?

Bliss Layer

- Who are you when you are fully yourself in that situation?
- If there were no restrictions, who would you be?

EXERCISE: PAY ATTENTION INSIDE

When you are not engaged in the present moment, you are no longer connected with yourself nor with your coachee. The next time you feel unsettled or as though "something is wrong", take the time to pay attention inside and:

- Notice the flow of energy inside your body, and feel where it is free flowing or where there are blockages.
- Pinpoint exactly which emotion you feel and what has triggered that feeling.
- Feel your physical reactions to events and situations, and pinpoint exactly when that physical reaction began and what caused it.

EXERCISE: WALKING MEDITATION

If possible, choose a nature-based setting such as a walk in the forest, by a river or lake, or up a mountain trail. If that is not possible, you can do this exercise in your house or apartment.

General Tips

- Set aside 15 to 30 minutes for your walk.
- Take a moment to clear your mind.
- Turn off your music.
- Breathe deeply and center yourself before beginning the walk.

Before you start your walk, ask your unconscious mind a question* such as:

- "Can you help me to clarify (situation)?"
- "Can you help me to determine my next step in resolving (situation)?"
- "Can you help me understand what is bothering me about (situation)?"

  * Only focus on one question per meditation.

Set your question aside and begin your walk.

- Be fully present to your experience (not your question).
- Notice what you notice without judgment.
- Don't assume that you have your answer if you notice something intriguing right away.

- Stay present the whole time, continuing to notice what you observe.

At the end of your walk, write down or reflect on what you noticed. Consider what any metaphor(s) might mean to you and your current situation. You may have insights right away, or you may need to do another walk to clarify what came up.

EXERCISE

The next time you prepare to make a significant decision, take a moment to ask yourself a question related to each of the five layers. Notice how this affects your decision.

❝❝ A COACHING CONVERSATION

Notice how the coach orients the coachee to her feelings as well as the associated physiology and energy. The coach uses somatic awareness to guide the coachee towards the state she is seeking.

Coach: What would you like to focus on today?

Coachee: I am in a job right now that is not something I want to do, it is high stress and not good for my health, I want to transition to coaching, but it will take time to do that. What do I do in the interim?

Coach: You mentioned a few things – stress, transition, job you don't like…At the end of this meeting, what is it that you would like to take away with you?

Coachee: Peace for where I am at.

Coach: Being more at peace with the job you are currently in?

Coachee: Actually, I want to reduce stress or manage it better, so I am free to look for another job.

Coach: How will you know at the end of the meeting that you have gained more clarity around that?

Coachee: More peace in my body, and a few ideas on how to manage it better.

Coach: Tell me a bit more about the job you are currently in.

Coachee: It is a never-ending job, I am behind all the time, I have too few resources, I do the job of two people, it is like a fire-fighting job, I also have to resolve things for the future, it is high pressure, I can't turn it off, they expect me to look at emails at night.

Coach: (pause) You are pretty clear on the sources of your stress and your reaction to it. What would a wise person tell you about your situation?

Coachee: She would remind me to do things one step at a time, that I am human.

Coach: What else would she say?

Coachee: She would tell me to breathe.

Coach: What happens when you take that breath?

Coachee: It calms me.

Coach: Where do you feel the calm?

Coachee: It opens my chest, I feel more open.

Coach: What happens in your environment when you take that breath?

Coachee: I remind myself 'one step at a time'. It will make me calmer.

Coach: Where do you feel that calmness?

Coachee: In my chest.

Coach: If we can fast forward a couple of weeks, you don't know what to expect, what does it feel like having that inner calmness?

Coachee: More relaxed.

Coach: Describe that feeling.

Coachee: When you stand straighter, your shoulders are square, you feel more in control.

Coach: Whose shoulders are you talking about?

Coachee: Mine.

Coach: Describe how you are in 2 weeks.

Coachee: Calmer, peaceful, straighter, one step at a time.

Coach: Is there anything else you notice in that picture? What is happening with the people around you?

Coachee: I work from home...my energy would be better.

Coach: How does your home feel?

Coachee: I feel calmer.

Coach: Is there anything else you are noticing, when you take a breath, shoulders square?

Coachee: I just feel calmer, more able.

Coach: Who are you when you are calmer, more able?

Coachee: I am more centered, more resourceful. It's just a job. It is not all of who I am. I need to keep it in perspective.

Coach: What would you need to help you get that calmness, serenity the next time you turn on that computer?

Coachee: The mantra, one step at a time, breathe in, breathe out. It's just a job.

Coach: How will you remember this?

Coachee: I can see it.

Coach: How is your body feeling now?

Coachee: Peaceful.

Coach: Is there anything else that you need?

Coachee: No.

Coach: We started the meeting talking about how you want to feel. You are considering different career paths, how does this fit in?

Coachee: Managing stress better helps me look at alternative jobs.

Coach: What are your next steps?

Coachee: The mantra, one step at a time, breathe in, breathe out. It's just a job.

”

SUMMARY

- Leaders must become connected with their feelings, emotions and intuition to access their full resourcefulness.
- We all have intuition and natural instincts available to help guide our decisions and actions.
- The body never lies and will continue to react to its circumstances — regardless of the logic we impose on it.
- Developing somatic intelligence includes learning to:
  - Feel and identify emotions
  - Recognize and interpret our "gut reaction" or intuition
  - Be present to our emotions, without needing to cover them or change them to something "better" or different
  - Read our own and other people's body language
- There are five layers to the self:
  - Physical
  - Energetic
  - Mental/emotional
  - Wisdom/intuition
  - Bliss/authentic self
- Somatic coaching allows the coach to connect with the coachee and allows the coachee to connect with herself more deeply.
- Somatic awareness helps the coachee understand how her thoughts affect her physically, emotionally and energetically.

Part 2

The 4-Step CARA Coaching Model

CHAPTER 4 - CONNECTION

"Meditation is not a way of making your mind quiet. It's a way of entering into the quiet that's already there — buried under the 50,000 thoughts the average person thinks every day."
Deepak Chopra

I am a task-focused person who is naturally introverted, so it took me a few years to appreciate the value of connection in business relationships. Most people like my high productivity; however, it can feel clinical to people who are extroverted and relationship-oriented.

My views about connecting with others did not change overnight; they were influenced by my observations of — and experiences with — people who are masterful at creating connections with others. These people take the time to get to know their co-workers at an intimate level, without invading their privacy or crossing corporate boundaries. For these types of people, connection is not just a formula for success — they genuinely care about others and want to understand who they are and what is important to them.

PARTNERSHIP

In a 3-legged race, if one of the partners is faster and forces her partner to take a longer or quicker stride, what is most likely to happen is that they will both fall over. To get to the end of the race, both partners need to coordinate their steps to stay in sync with each other. The same rule applies to business relationships.

Leaders are often accustomed to directing or controlling conversations with their employees; however, in a coaching conversation, the coach and coachee are considered partners in the relationship, with the coach allowing the coachee to set the pace.

In a business setting, it is natural to have predetermined boundaries and parameters that coachees must adhere to. Once those are met, the coach needs be open to unexpected outcomes. To do this the coach asks questions that invite discovery but do not force a specific outcome.

"If you judge people, you have no time to love them."
Mother Teresa

REFLECTION

How do you feel about letting your coachee (employee) set the pace for your discussion?

How do you feel about setting boundaries, then being completely open to the outcome of the discussion?

SAFETY

In a work setting, discussions rarely have intimacy. The coach approach changes this by offering a safe approach to creating deeper connections. As you learn and begin implementing the coach approach, you will notice that conversations become warmer and trust develops as a result. The coach's and participant's body language is noticeably more relaxed.

Coaching discussions aim to create a personal connection so that the coachee feels safe enough to be vulnerable and take risks. This type of connection requires a combination of confidentiality, trust and mutual respect. To achieve these, the coachee must feel that the coach is non-judgmental and that she won't use the coaching discussions against her in the future.

"People don't care how much you know until they know how much you care."
John C. Maxwell

The coach approach offers a safe approach to creating deeper connections.

ENCOURAGING CONNECTION

While a connection cannot be forced, there are many things that you can do to encourage a connection with your coachee. These include:

- Showing a genuine interest in your coachees' well-being
- Being trustworthy
- Creating a safe and inviting environment for your meeting
- Ensuring 100% confidentiality
- Having excellent sensory acuity so that you can get in sync with your coachee
- Having a process, but letting your coachee set the pace
- Being open and non-judgmental
- Being friendly and engaging, but above all, being yourself

"While it is simple to practice mindfulness, it is not necessarily easy."
John Kabat-Zinn

Mike is a graduate of our leadership coaching program. He is the CEO of a children's charity, and his success at fundraising is a direct result of his ability to create meaningful relationships with others.

"For me it is all about relationships, not only in business but in life. I feel in my heart that I'm placed on this planet to serve mankind and give back wherever possible. Starting new and stewarding old relationships come(s) from a knowing, or core belief, that we are all miracles of having the gift of life. In any relationship situation I can adapt to the needs of others. What that produces is a calm connection (not having to put on a show) by being myself (I am enough) and allowing the relationship opportunities to flow naturally. This approach can rapidly bring down the walls that might impede the progress of the relationship. From there I allow my intuition to ask good questions, have empathy where needed and just be there for the individual I'm engaged with."

Mike

COACHING ASSUMPTIONS

Your frame of mind is key to coaching, and the way you think about the coachee impacts the mood and outcome of the resulting conversation. Consider implementing some or all of the following assumptions:

- "You cannot **not** communicate. Notice what is left unsaid or is communicated through body language.
- The words we use are our interpretation of events and things, they are not the event or item that they represent.
- Acknowledge that each person is influenced by, and operates from, their own model of the world.
- The system (person) with the most flexibility of behavior will have the most influence on the system.
- The meaning of communication received is the response it produces.
- There is no failure — only feedback.
- Every behavior has a positive intention.
- Every behavior is useful in some context.
- Everyone is always doing what they believe is right.
- The behavior or decision that an individual makes is the best choice available to them given the circumstances as they see it.
- There are no unresourceful people, only unresourceful states.
- You are in charge of your mind and therefore your results.
- Behavior and change are to be evaluated in terms of context and ecology.

We are not suggesting that the above assumptions are the truth, but we do suggest that by acting as if these assumptions are true, we have found that excellent results are easier to achieve."

(Excerpted with permission from the NLP Partners, NLP Basic Practitioner Manual.)

*"I used to think I was lacking in intelligence because I speak slower than most people. I did not think I had a lot to say. When I started learning the **Coaching Assumptions** it helped me to like myself and stop putting myself down. I started applying them early on. They were like a lifeline for me. They allowed me to accept myself for who I am."*

Sandra

"To a mind that is still, the whole Universe surrenders."
Chuang Tzu

CONNECT WITH YOURSELF

It is not possible to connect with someone else if you are not first connected with yourself. This involves learning how to pay attention to your physical body, thoughts, emotions, energy and intuition. When you can do this, you will be able to gather and process information on multiple levels. Your intuition will guide the type of questions you ask, the pace at which you ask them and enable you to take advantage of your intuition.

One of the simplest ways to connect with yourself is by meditating. Dr. Kabat-Zinn, a leading researcher at the Stress Reduction Clinic at the University of Massachusetts Medical Center and author of numerous mindfulness books including *Full Catastrophe Living* and *Using the Wisdom of Your Body and Mind to Face Stress, Pain and Illness*, has helped thousands of people learn simple meditation techniques. He tells his students that they have only *moments* to live, meaning that you should be present for every moment. With practice, these moments soon increase in duration, enabling you to live more mindfully.

Being mindful can be both simple and much more difficult than you might think. When you are mindful, you pay attention to the present moment and experience the sensations, emotions, thoughts and insights that arise — without getting sidetracked. As easy as that sounds, many people find that they have lost the ability to live in the moment. Instead, they focus their thoughts on the past and the future, while barely noticing what is going on inside and around them.

Meditation and mindfulness have benefits that can be difficult to appreciate until you actually experience them. In addition to helping you become calmer and more focused, meditation can also help you to get more in touch with your real self — which is one of its primary goals. Meditation helps you to go inside yourself and experience emotions and feelings that you may have neglected, ignored or even been unable to deal with in the past.

When you slow down and stop multi-tasking, you have the opportunity to notice the endless thoughts that pop into your head. Being mindful during everyday activities allows you to notice the thought patterns that dominate your thinking. You also notice your feelings in various situations and recognize what is different between being in calming and peaceful situations and being in stressful, angry or sad situations. By observing yourself from a more objective perspective, you can gain insight into why you feel the way you do — eventually noticing triggers, beliefs, values and other filters that you use.

First, you notice what is going on inside of you. Then, pay attention to what is going inside of your coachee.

"In the West, we tend to underestimate the importance of a person's way of being. We focus instead on his or her knowledge, skills or techniques."
Robert Hargrove

EXERCISE: MINDFULNESS

Be deliberately mindful the next time you do a routine task such as washing the dishes, loading or unloading the dishwasher, gardening, etc. While you are performing this activity, keep your mind focused on the activity and notice your thoughts, physical sensations, feelings and energy.

If your mind wanders, bring your focus back to the activity.

REFLECTION

Where did your mind wander to?

Was it hard or easy to keep your focus on the activity?

MEDITATING

When you first start meditating, you often catch yourself getting drawn to other thoughts or images before consciously pulling your attention back to your breath, mantra or meditative movement, only to have your mind wander yet again. It can seem as though you are never going to catch on to meditating. But if you persist, you will find that, at some point, you are able to notice the thoughts and images more objectively with the awareness that these are only diversions. This allows you to acknowledge the thoughts without getting drawn into them. Or — at the very least — it prevents you from being as consumed with these thoughts as you normally might be.

Becoming more aware of the sea of thoughts constantly moving through your head may initially make you feel as though you are going backwards in your progression towards calmness and peacefulness; however, the simple acknowledgment of your thoughts is a very useful step in the process. By allowing yourself to observe and acknowledge your thoughts, you then have the opportunity to change them.

EXERCISE: SIMPLE BREATHING

- Sit upright in your chair or stand.
- Place your feet hip-width apart, flat on the ground.
- Place your hands in your lap or let them hang freely.
- Relax your shoulders.
- Close your eyes.
- Notice your breath going in and out.
- Pay attention to your breath for a few minutes.
- When your mind wanders, simply bring your attention back to your breath.

REFLECTION

How do you feel after focusing on your breath for a few minutes?

Did your mind wander? What did it wander to?

CENTER YOURSELF

Many coaches find themselves flustered or drawing a blank when they first begin working with coachees. This is sometimes because they have not taken the time to let go of what they were previously concentrating on and, consequently, are not present to the coaching experience. Sometimes they are nervous and have trouble calming down. In either case, when this happens, they find that their thoughts just do not seem to flow easily.

When you are calm, questions flow naturally. Conversely, when you overthink your questions or anticipate where the conversation will go, it feels much harder and you end up doing more work than the coachee. If you find yourself in this state, slow down the process and re-center yourself.

One of the simplest ways to calm and focus yourself before a coaching meeting is to practice abdominal breathing; this is as simple as sitting down and spending a few minutes focusing inwards on your breath. Abdominal breathing helps you get more oxygen into your lungs, gives you something to focus your mind on and slows your heart and breathing rates. This in turn helps you to be calmer and more focused during your coaching meeting. Although it takes a bit of practice in the beginning, it will soon feel natural and effortless.

> Tip
>
> If your coachee seems rushed or flustered, it can be useful to take a few moments together to breathe deeply and relax before continuing the meeting.

When you focus inward on your breath, you will notice that your breaths become deeper and slower, thereby calming your nervous system. If you practice abdominal breathing for a few minutes before your coaching meeting, you will notice that you are calmer and better able to focus. During the meeting, you will be more in touch with yourself — and your coachee, as well.

The coach's best allies are calmness and focus.

"Tension is who you think you should be. Relaxation is who you are."
Chinese Proverb

EXERCISE: ABDOMINAL BREATHING

- Sit up tall with one hand on your navel, the other on your knee.
- Relax your belly.
- Close your eyes.
- Inhale deeply through your nose so that the hand over your navel is pushed outward (your belly should swell like a balloon).
- Exhale deeply through your nose and notice how your navel comes back in towards your spine.
- Relax your belly even more.
- Breathe deeply without forcing the breath.
- Continue for a couple of minutes.

" A COACHING CONVERSATION

Notice how the coach introduces a limit to the venting — and a way to calm down afterwards.

....

Coachee: I am so mad. I can't believe she did that. It was my idea. I wish I had said something during the meeting. She is always stealing my ideas and

passing them off as her own....
Coach: (makes a time-out signal) May I suggest that we set a time limit for
you to vent, then take a moment to center ourselves before we carry on with
the meeting?
Coachee: Okay. I really do need to vent a bit more. Is five minutes ok?
Coach: Okay. Five minutes, then we center ourselves.
....

"Be the change
you want to see
in the world."
Mahatma Gandhi

ESTABLISH TRUST

Until trust has been built, a meaningful conversation can't take
place. To create an atmosphere of trust, you need to offer a
safe space, build rapport and assure your coachee of 100%
confidentiality.

Safe Space

If you are meeting face to face with your coachee, choose a
location that is tidy, comfortable, an appropriate temperature, free
from distractions (no phones, computers and other technological
devices) and private (behind closed doors and soundproof). Some
coachees are happy to meet in public places like coffee shops —
let your coachee make this decision.

Help your coachee feel welcome and safe by letting her choose her
own seat (if appropriate). Avoid sitting behind a desk, or directly
beside or in front of your coachee. When possible, sit near your
coachee at a diagonal, with adequate personal space between you.
This helps to facilitate a conversation rather than a confrontation.

Take a few minutes to calm and center yourself before your
meeting using deep, slow abdominal breathing or a meditation of
your choice. You can do this before your coachee arrives, or with
her before you begin your meeting.

Create Rapport

Rapport is the foundation for any meaningful conversation. You achieve rapport by being responsive to your coachee's words, energy, emotions and feelings. Rapport is achieved when your coachee feels comfortable, safe and in sync with you.

Once built, rapport needs to be maintained. If you abruptly change topics, body language, tone of voice or become distracted, you may lose rapport with your coachee.

Match and Mirror

If you match and mirror your coachee's posture, breathing, tone, cadence and selection of words, you will create deeper rapport. This does not mean that you *copy* your coachee's body language (because it might look as though you are mocking her). Rather, it means that you get in sync while maintaining your authenticity. If she is sitting, sit. If she is standing, stand.

Leading a State Change

If your coachee is excited or agitated and speaking very quickly, and you are speaking very slowly and calmly, she may not feel that you are connected. Instead, connect with her by meeting her where she is at by speaking more quickly than normal. Once you achieve rapport, you can then start slowing down. If you are in rapport, and don't change the pace abruptly, you will notice that your coachee also slows down. As you do this, pay attention to your coachee so that you don't break rapport. This is how you lead your coachee to a state that is more conducive to coaching.

Confidentiality

Your coachee must be assured of 100% confidentiality and that the conversation will not be used against her in the future. This can be accomplished via a written or verbal agreement. You may still need to take baby steps to demonstrate your trustworthiness, so let your coachee set the pace for how much she is willing to disclose.

Tips to Establish Trust, Rapport and Connection

- When you are with your coachee, be fully present for her. This may mean that you need to take some time before your meeting to calm and clear your mind.
- Relax. Don't think up questions while your coachee is talking.
- Take pauses and offer insightful questions, using 100% of your attention.
- Use active listening and set your own beliefs and values aside. Listen to what is important for your coachee — even if it is not the way *you* think or act.
- Trust your intuition. If you are relaxed and pay attention to your coachee, the right question will come up at the right time.
- Limit note taking. Focus on your coachee.
- If you find yourself working too hard, relax, breathe and slow down the coaching process.
- Take the time to transition from what you were working on prior to the coaching meeting by using abdominal breathing or some other method to calm and focus you.

SENSORY ACUITY

Your ability to notice changes in yourself and others through your senses is a critical part of effective communication. When your sensory acuity is developed, you notice:

- Feedback that indicates the extent to which you are on or off target in communicating your message
- Other people's reactions to situations/stimuli
- Your reactions to situations/stimuli

Quick Facts about Sensory Acuity

When you communicate with others, 55% of the meaning of your message is conveyed through your body language, 38% through your voice tonality and only 7% through the actual words that you choose. [5]

When coaching, listen for the words but, more importantly, notice changes in body language, tone of voice, cadence of speech and other subtle signs that demonstrate what your coachee is really communicating. If you pay careful attention, you might also notice energy and emotional shifts. These are clues to coachable moments or situations.

Body Language

Connection requires a union between two or more people — the deeper the connection, the deeper the potential results. When you are connected with another person, you naturally feel a closeness and empathy for her. You are able to notice changes in her body language, intuit her feelings and hear what is unsaid beneath her words.

---

5   Mehrabian A and SR Ferris, *Inference of Attitudes from Nonverbal Communication in Two Channels,* Journal of Consulting Psychology, 1967 Jun;31(3):248-52.

A person's body language, voice characteristics and choice of words reveal a great deal about how she reacts to a situation. Body language includes facial expressions, gestures, posture, breathing rate, etc. Your coachee's face alone provides a wealth of information: notice her eyes (distant or focused), facial expression (relaxed or tense) and skin color (flushed, pale or the person's normal color).

Other body movements to look for include: speed of movement (quick or slow), toe or finger tapping, fidgeting, crossing of arms, leaning forward or backwards, proximity of the person (crowding you or too far away), sighs and pauses.

With practice you can become skilled at reading body language. This gives you valuable feedback when you present and receive information, and allows you to make adjustments to your presentations in "real time." For example, if the coachee looks confused, you can ask if she needs clarification. If she looks bored, you can change your approach to re-engage her. If you are on the receiving end of a message, you can evaluate if the message being passed is sincere.

Don't assume that you know what your coachee's body language means. Ask.

Notice:

- Skin tone/color
- Breathing rate
- Posture
- Gestures
- Facial expressions
- Blinking

Voice Tonality

Using the same words, changes in voice tonality can convey very different meanings. Notice:

- Tone (indicates the mood of the message)
- Tempo (speed)
- Timbre (quality)
- Volume (loudness)

Words

When speaking, ensure that your choice of words is appropriate to the education and background of the person that you are speaking with. When listening, notice:

- Key words
- Words that describe beliefs and values
- Words that describe feelings or energy
- Metaphors
- Pauses

66 A COACHING CONVERSATION

Notice how the coach keeps asking questions to uncover the deeper issue without getting side-tracked. This conversation is longer than the others I've included in this book; however, it demonstrates beautifully what can unfold when there is trust and the coach stays curious, without getting attached to a specific outcome. Notice also how the coach takes advantage of the seed metaphor presented by the coachee and weaves it back into the conversation to gain closure.

Coach: What do you want to focus on?

Coachee: I have been so focused on my health, I am finally feeling better, but I am feeling bored with my life right now. I am not sure what to do about it. I have been busy running my business. I think it is a seven-year itch. I love teaching, but I am not thrilled with the management. I just feel 'naah', been there, done that. I have someone interested in buying the business. She is also interested in becoming a partner. My relationship is 'blaah', nothing is exciting me.

Coach: (big breath) You have a lot going on. I am hearing bored, selling your business, potential business partner, husband. What is the most important thing to focus on?

Coachee: My husband. Everything else could fall away, but that is important. My family is more of a priority than my business. I am bored with my husband, too. That is more serious.

Coach: What would you like to explore about that today?

Coachee: We are in counseling. He has issues, but I know it is not all him. It is like, 'yeah, he's there,' but I don't feel the same way about him as I used to. I don't know if it is possible to feel the same way about him.

Coach: Is that what you want to focus on today?

Coachee: (sigh) Not really. I am working on that with a marriage counselor. My husband has issues. I am just trying to embrace this confused state that I am in. I am in a state of flux. I get excited about selling my business, then I get in a panic about selling it. I don't know what I want to do when I grow up. I am obviously going through a transition. In hindsight, I know that these things become clear. I am going through menopause, too. Two kids just moved back in. My life is a mess....Not a mess. I am happy, but I don't have a lot of clarity.

Coach: I am hearing a lot of confusion. Menopause, husband, selling business, kids moving back in. (Pause) If there was one thing that would bring relief, what would be the best thing to focus on today?

Coachee: Working on me being okay with not knowing whether this relationship will last another 10-20 years, okay with not knowing about the business. I like to have control. (Laughs).

Coach: (laughs) I get that! What is good about embracing uncertainty?

Coachee: The thought that I have control is ridiculous. I need to surrender. Let things evolve as they should. It is like when a seed is about to sprout. It is where I am at now.

Coach: Imagine what it feels like....a seed about to sprout. What does that feel like?

Coachee: Tension.

Coachee: When a seed is about to sprout, what does it need?

Coachee: Water, sunshine.

Coach: Anything else?

Coachee: Shit! (Laughs) Compost for nourishment.

Coach: When a seed is disturbed, it is difficult to grow. Does that have meaning for you?

Coachee: Yes, it needs peace and rest.

Coach: What does this tell you about your situation?

Coachee: Before the seed sprouts, it has to crack open. I just have to stay grounded. Stay the course. Drink water, get sunshine! Do restorative yoga. My God, yes! That is plain as the nose on my face. I need to get my bolsters out and lie down. I have not had energy for so long, and I was in a fog. Now that I have energy, I feel like I should be doing things that I have not been able to do. I have been burning up all of my energy.

Coach: It takes energy to crack the seed.

Coachee: Yes.

Coach: How does the shit fit in — the compost?

Coachee: My family. I have so many good friends who are like family. I have a lot of support from different people.

Coach: How will they support your growth?

Coachee: We support each other's growth. We are all on the same path, and we are there for each other. I give a lot, but I also receive a lot. (laughs) I feel like a nut about to sprout.

Coach: What do you need most right now?

Coachee: Just be okay. Stop trying to have the answers. Be ok not having the answers. Trust. Everything will be just fine.

Coach: What is that like?

Coachee: Tough. I give this advice, but I don't take it. I know. I can't do it for myself. I like the idea of the yoga. Be still. Ride the wave. When I am still, the right answer will come. I have not been still since I have had energy again.

Coach: When you allow yourself to be still, what picture emerges?

Coachee: Reclined bound angle pose. It is a vulnerable position, but heart opening and fully supported.

Coach: Vulnerable, heart opening, fully supported. How does that sound?

Coachee: (mmmm) Good

Coach: If you could be vulnerable, heart open, fully supported….what will emerge then?

Coachee: A lot of love. When I am feeling unsafe, I close that down. That is where I prefer to live, the place of love. The doors have been closed lately.

Coach: Is there something unsafe?

Coachee: My husband, female friends, he has betrayed my trust.

Coach: Is that the underlying issue? Trust?

Coachee: If I go down underneath that feeling, it is security. I depend on him financially. Where will I go? I will be on the street. The fear of being a bag lady. Fear of abandonment. I know intellectually that won't happen, but the human instinct that drives that. I was a single mother for so many years. I said I would never be financially dependent on a man again. It was big for me to trust. To let my husband pay the bills. Now I am not liking that feeling of being dependent. It impacts my decision making. The issue is embracing the uncertainty.

Coach: It seems like it is bringing up security and a fear in you.

Coachee: That is why I was thinking of selling the business.

Coach: What is most important?

Coachee: My family. My kids. All of us. I have been rich. I have been poor. I am always fine. The money always works out. But it is more than that. It is the integrity of my family. We have had history together. I don't want to screw that up.

Coach: We started talking about this place where there are many things. But there seems to be a driver underneath, the security. What is the best way to use the rest of our time together?

Coachee: I have had this security thing. I know it is a myth. It keeps coming up. How do I keep that from rearing its ugly head? What do I do?

Coach: Great question…

Coachee: I have lived this so many times. Why am I learning this lesson? I want to be done with this one.

Coach: Is there a lesson to be learned from the seed?

Coachee: It is the seed's destiny to grow.

Coach: How does the seed know its destiny?

Coachee: That burning desire. It has to happen. It is not an option.

Coach: There are built-in instincts, right?

Coachee: It is like a deeper inner wisdom.

Coach: How does that relate to you?

Coachee: I need to ramp up my meditation. Be mindful.

Coach: How do you listen to your instincts, destiny, whatever is programmed into you?

Coachee: My destiny is clear. To teach. To continue to study. I know this.

Coach: How do you know?

Coachee: A burning desire and when I am doing it, it feels right. An effortless flow.

Coach: What is that telling you?

Coachee: Stop trying to push a rope up a hill.

Coach: Tell me more about that.

Coachee: I stopped meditation once I started feeling good. I need to meditate more. Pay attention inside.

Coach: Moving forward, what will be different?

Coachee: I need to come back to myself. My practice. The right path will *show itself.*

Coach: Is there anything specific you want to do differently?

Coachee: Be more open. Not get aggravated by my 'teachers' — my family members.

Coach: If you are not aggravated, you are…

Coachee: Realize that they are not deliberately trying to irritate me.

Coach: I have heard….come back to yourself, practice, be okay with your teachers, what else?

Coachee: Being present. Quit worrying about the future. Today.

Coach: When you look now at your situation now, how are you feeling?

Coachee: I am just going to worry about this afternoon.

Coach: Worry?

Coachee: I am going to take care of my garden. **"**

SUMMARY

- Choose a safe meeting place and time for your coaching meetings.
- Create rapport and build trust with your coachee prior to engaging in deep coaching work.
- Relax and be present during the coaching meetings.
- Limit note taking. Focus on the coachee.
- Center yourself prior to the coaching meeting. This allows you to be fully present and open to listening to your intuition. It also allows you to pay attention to your reactions to your coachee.
- Create an atmosphere of trust and respect.
- If you feel flustered or that the meeting is going too quickly, take a moment to re-center yourself and slow the process down (while maintaining rapport with the coachee).
- Assure your coachee of 100% confidentiality.

Chapter 5 - Awareness

It is natural for coaches to want to help others achieve success. We want to provide value and help our coachees get results as soon as possible. If we try to do too much at once, however, it can have the opposite effect. Because of people's limited capacity to focus on and absorb new information, the best service that we can provide to our coachees is to help them focus on the most important topic in their life at that time.

When I first started coaching, I facilitated epic meetings — sometimes more than two hours in duration. I wanted the coachee to leave feeling like she got good value from our time together. Now that I know what a good coach can accomplish in 30 minutes or less, I cringe when I think of those lengthy meetings. Not only were they too long, but we accomplished so many things that it may have been difficult for the coachee to process all of the information.

I now recommend shorter, focused discussions which result in a clear outcome. This approach allows the coachee to commit to actions that move her towards her desired outcome and keep her energy directed to what is most important.

AWARENESS

Many people today live such busy lives that they are no longer present to their thoughts and emotions. They may know that something is wrong but are not able to put their finger on the issue. Or, they may know what is wrong but be unwilling or unable to address the root cause.

In the awareness step you help your coachee expand her understanding of the topic. For best results, ensure that your coachee is working on the **one** most important topic at hand or you limit the value of your coaching meeting.

> The goal of the awareness step is to understand the history of the topic, what is important about it and what the coachee wants to gain from the meeting.

The focus is on understanding the current situation in order to create a framework for the future. For example, if the coachee begins with:

Coachee: I am feeling incompetent at my job.

You help the coachee to become clear on what that means and how it is affecting her or those around her. If the coach keeps asking questions about exactly how incompetent the client feels and how bad that makes her feel, the coachee can become so dejected that she is unable to imagine any other possibilities.

Mike is the CEO of Make a Wish® Eastern Ontario, an organization that grants the wishes of children between the ages of three and seventeen with life-threatening medical conditions.

"The leadership coaching has helped me in many ways, and I would like to share one example with you.

Last year I approached a potential donor who was ready to commit to providing a wish for one child. After our discussion, he reflected and contributed one wish per month for a total donation of $120,000. A few years ago, I would have been happy to settle with the sponsorship of the one wish. In fact, I would have been thrilled to receive the donation.

When I approach potential donors, I take the time to truly understand the donor's needs and use my expertise in coaching to find a solution that fulfills those needs. I always focus on creating win-win agreements. If one person feels that they were taken advantage of, the relationship will fail. The person who feels like they gave away too much may not want to negotiate the next time around and that works both ways—in business and personally.

With the donor who contributed one wish per month, I used questioning to find out that he wanted to give back because of what he witnessed as a young man. I also found out that his business had a goal of giving back to the community for corporate responsibility. By fully exploring those two needs, he came to the conclusion that his organization could support a donation of one wish per month. This met his needs and provided a huge boost to the Make a Wish® foundation of Eastern Ontario."

ILLUMINATING BLIND SPOTS

While it is tempting to *tell* the coachee what areas she needs to work on, it is preferable for the coachee to uncover her own blind spots, at her own pace, with the assistance of artful questioning. In athletics, coaches sometimes use video cameras to help illuminate problems for their athletes. A running coach might show his athlete a video of the athlete running, and then ask her what she is noticing about her stride or posture. If the athlete does not notice the problem, the coach might point out the problem to her or show the athlete a video of someone who is performing the movement correctly. By becoming aware of the problem, the athlete can then learn to optimize her movements.

As a coach, your job is to find creative ways to hold up the mirror to promote learning and growth rather than self-criticism.

❝ A COACHING CONVERSATION

....

Coachee: I told my son that he needs to leave the house if he can't follow the rules.

Coach: How did he respond?

Coachee: It is maddening. The rules are so simple to follow. He keeps saying that we are 'kicking him out'. He does not seem to realize that he just needs to follow the rules. We aren't 'kicking him out'.

Coach: If you look through his eyes, how do you interpret your message?

Coachee: (pause) When I see it from this perspective, I think he feels like he is in a no-win situation. We are imposing rules rather than discussing them with him. He feels like he is getting too old to be told what to do.

Coach: And...

Coachee: I think we need to have a different conversation with him. ❞

.....

BE PREPARED TO BE SURPRISED

You may be surprised by what surfaces when you begin clarifying the topic. Sometimes it morphs into another topic, and at other times it creates unexpected understandings that lead to change.

"The main thing is to keep the main thing the main thing."
Stephen Covey

❝ A COACHING CONVERSATION

....

Coachee: I want to focus on increasing my business.

Coach: (pause)

Coachee: I hate marketing and sales, but I need to do more of it. I want to learn to be more effective at it.

Coach: What is going on for you when you think of marketing and sales?

Coachee: I hate pushy sales people. I don't want to be like that.

Coach: I am feeling a lot of emotion. What is underneath that?

Coachee: The thought of doing sales causes a lot of stress. I'm just not good at it, and I don't want people to think I am annoying.

Coach: What is the opposite of stressful and annoying?

Coachee: Calm and useful.

Coach: Would it benefit you to find a sales style where you feel calm and useful?

Coachee: That is a lot more appealing.

.... ❞

COACHES ARE OBJECTIVE OBSERVERS

Do not allow yourself to get drawn into your coachee's story. As the coach, you are an objective observer with the goal of assisting your coachee in the expansion of her understanding about the topic. If you don't understand her words or descriptions, that is perfectly fine. Your role is to make sure that *she* understands these descriptions.

Even if you think you have had a similar experience to your

coachee, let it go. This is not about you. You may create confusion and possibly even lose rapport by introducing your meaning to your coachee's story.

If your coachee is having difficulty exploring her situation objectively, repeating back the coachee's words can help the coachee understand her situation with more clarity.

UNDERSTANDING BEHAVIOR PATTERNS

The awareness step helps the coachee understand her behavior patterns and identify where else in her life she uses those patterns. For example, if your coachee discusses her difficulty in asking her boss for what she needs, you may be curious about:

- The underlying pattern (i.e. is it just about *how* to ask for what she needs, or is there a deeper pattern such as not feeling *worthy* of asking for what she needs)
- Where *else* this pattern manifests itself
- What the *benefit* to the coachee is in continuing this pattern

The coachee can then identify more specifically what resource is missing in order to achieve the desired outcome.

THE MEETING AGREEMENT

A coaching meeting requires an agenda to ensure that the conversation is productive, and not just a friendly chat. In coaching, this is called the "meeting agreement." You help your coachee:

- Identify <u>one</u> **topic** that she wants to focus on
- Identify how to determine if the meeting is successful (measuring the **outcome**)
- Be precise and focused in her thoughts and discussions

"People become really quite remarkable when they start thinking that they can do things. When they believe in themselves they have the first secret of success."
Norman Vincent Peale

The Topic

Coachees sometimes begin the meeting with a topic that is not the deepest issue affecting them. Instead, they present something safe or superficial. At other times, coachees begin the meeting with several things that they want to work on.

Your job is to assist your coachee in clarifying and narrowing down the discussion to the one, specific, topic that your coachee wants to focus on. At the end of the meeting, she will develop a clear resolution for this one, specific, topic.

There are times when the entire meeting is devoted to clarifying the topic and desired outcome. This is not wasted time. The simple act of creating awareness regarding the topic provides value to the coachee. The discussion provides focus, and brings to the surface those underlying thoughts that were previously unsaid or that the coachee was unwilling to acknowledge.

" A COACHING CONVERSATION (TOPIC)

Coach: What would you like to focus on today?
Coachee: Right from the first day of my new job I knew something was wrong. I should have listened to that feeling. Now I can't leave. I feel like I should be able to make this work, but I am so stressed when I drive to work. It is affecting my sleep and my health.
Coach: I heard several things: listening to intuition; being stressed; health issues; something wrong with your job. What is the most important thing to focus on today?
Coachee: The most important thing right now is understanding if I can make this job work, or if I should look for a new job. **(Topic)**
....

The Meeting Outcome

Ask your coachee what her desired outcome is for the meeting. The outcome is not something that she will "get" sometime after the meeting, but rather it is a way to measure what specifically she will have at the end of the meeting that she does not have now. Desired outcomes can include:

- A plan
- Clarity on the topic
- A feeling (like confidence)
- A vision

❝ A COACHING CONVERSATION (OUTCOME)

.....

Coach: What would you like to have at the end of this conversation that you don't have now?

Coachee: I want to know what is bothering me about this job. I don't want to just quit, otherwise I might end up with the same problems at another job. **(Outcome)**

Coach: How will you know if you have what you need?

Coachee: I will understand the underlying issue and know if I can make some changes where I am now or if I need to find a new job.

Coach: What specifically will tell you that you have the understanding that you need?

Coachee: A feeling of certainty. I will have clarity.

Coach: Where will you have that feeling?

Coachee: Everywhere. I will feel strong and clear. **(Measurement of the outcome***)*

....

At the end of the meeting, you can check in to see if she is feeling strong and clear.

REFLECTION

How comfortable are you in being tenacious to negotiate clear meeting agreements?

How will you know when it is time to interrupt your coachee if she is unfocused and expansive?

EXERCISE

Over the next week, use questions to negotiate a meeting agreement.

CASE STUDY

Anne arrived at the coaching meeting with a lot on her mind. She wanted to focus on expanding her business but also mentioned that she was distracted by several personal things. She was a week late in signing a separation agreement with her husband and was worried about her son who was quite angry about the separation. She was also one year behind in filing her tax return.

When asked, "What is most important?" it was clear that she needed to focus on her personal issues before discussing the expansion of her business.

SAMPLE AWARENESS QUESTIONS

To keep your coachee on track and on-time, ask:

- What do you want to focus your time on today?
- What do you want to resolve or gain clarity on today?
- How will you know when your topic is fully resolved (or you have achieved the clarity you want)?
- Of the three things you want to work on, what is most important right now?
- What is important?
- What is really important?
- How is this holding you back?
- Really?
- How do you know that?
- What is the underlying issue?
- How could you simplify that?
- What is the truth here?
- If you could see your situation from an observer's position, what would you notice?
- You have _____ minutes. Can you give me an idea of where you are at now?

Identifying the most important topic provides significant value to the coachee. It can help remove emotional associations from the issue, and start moving your coachee towards a resolution.

Periodically check in with your coachee:

- Are you on the right track?
- Are you working on the most important thing?
- Is there anything more important to focus on?
- Is this the most important topic?
- Is this the underlying topic?

"We are continually faced by great opportunities brilliantly disguised as insoluble problems."
Unknown

ACTIVE LISTENING

Active listening means that your attention is on your coachee. You are not reading emails, scanning Facebook or cleaning your office. When you are fully present, you do not formulate questions while your coachee is speaking or plan ahead to where you want the conversation to go. You simply listen to the words being said while paying attention to the subtleties of your coachee's body language, voice changes and energy shifts.

When you actively listen, you encourage your coachee to talk about her challenges and opportunities without giving advice. When you speak, ask purposeful questions to help her clarify, develop new resources or move into action. Questions should be short and precise, with the intention of moving your coachee towards her desired outcome.

Mirroring

Mirroring is repeating back the speaker's words without generalizing, distorting or simplifying in order to help the speaker clarify her message. By hearing her own words repeated back to her, she can reflect on the words and then clarify as needed. Hearing her own words allows the speaker to present her message more objectively and precisely.

Based on our unique backgrounds, experiences and learning styles, we associate different meanings with seemingly simple or straightforward words. When we speak aloud or communicate through writing, we translate and simplify our thoughts into words in order to convey a much broader and deeper picture. We generalize some concepts, and distort others while trying to simplify the message, or try to fit the message into words. To do this, we delete information in order to simplify our message. Only the speaker knows exactly what she is trying to say.

If the recipient of the information creates her own meaning by substituting her own words for those of the speaker, the message can quickly lose its original meaning. Remember: you are not responsible for understanding what your coachee is saying. Instead, you are responsible for helping your coachee understand what she is saying and how it is meaningful to her.

❝ A COACHING CONVERSATION (MIRRORING)

....

Coachee: I want to show up as an equal, so sometimes I assert myself to make a point.

Coach: You assert yourself as a way of showing up as an equal.

Coachee: I guess when I hear it that way, it's not just asserting myself. I need to show that I can contribute equally to the team.

Coach: Contributing equally to the team allows you to show up as an equal?

Coachee: Hmmm, maybe there are better ways to show up as an equal? ❞

....

Paraphrasing

Paraphrasing is a summarizing technique you can use to help a client clarify her message. In this case, you simplify the speaker's words to convey a concise meaning while attempting to preserve the meaning of the original message. This is especially useful if your client has been talking a lot and you want her to be more focused.

Paraphrasing is less precise than mirroring and runs the risk of influencing your coachee if you put words into her mouth.

❝ A COACHING CONVERSATION (PARAPHRASING)

....

Coachee: I am torn about my business partnership. Last year I felt like I could not work with one of my partners, so I formed a new company. Now, because of personal reasons, two of the new partners have left. I am thinking of changing partnership arrangements again. But I want to preserve my relationship with my current partner, even though I don't want to work directly with him anymore.

Coach: I am hearing that you want to take a fresh look at your business relationships.

Coachee: Yes, that is exactly right. I want to step back and take a look at what I need right now.

....

"

AWARENESS QUESTIONS

- What would you like to focus on today?
- What would you like to achieve today?
- What would you like to resolve today?
- What do you want?
- What does that mean?
- What does that feel like? Where do you feel it?
- What is important about that to you?
- When were you like that before?
- What's at risk?
- How does that resonate with you?
- What else?
- Does this interaction have a familiar ring to it?
- What is your contribution to this pattern?
- What can you do to stay on course?
- How do you know that?
- What else does that explain?
- Where else do you use that pattern?
- What is important?
- What is most important?
- What is the truth here?
- What is holding you back the most?
- What needs immediate attention?
- If you could see your situation from an observer's position, what would you notice?
- How is this holding you back?
- Is this the key issue?
- Is this the underlying issue?
- Can give you me one specific example of how this issue is affecting you?
- What opportunities are you missing?
- Can you be more specific?
- How specifically does this affect...?
- What do you want to accomplish?
- What outcomes do you want?

𝟔𝟔 A COACHING CONVERSATION

Note how the coach keeps asking questions that help the coachee to focus on what is important. At the beginning of the meeting, the coachee gives long, rambling answers. As she gets clear on her topic, her answers get shorter, and she gets more focused. Notice how the coach keeps feeding back the coachee's words to help her gain clarity.

Coach: What would you like to focus on today?

Coachee: The dilemma I have is making a decision about pursuing more of a self-employment model vs. a job. I have taken an in-between job. I want the freedom to pursue more of my passions. Today, I want to get clear on what I most want to pay attention to as I make decisions. I got a job offer yesterday, but I am not sure if it is right. I want to maintain the right balance, keep freedom to have the space that I need. I want to learn how to listen to the right voices inside me.

Coach: At face value self-employment vs. job seems pretty straightforward, but I wonder if there is something more to it than that?

Coachee: It is complicated. There are many factors that come into it. Safety and security vs. freedom come up. Both are important in different ways. Balance is important. Self-employment is more freeing, but it could be less free if I take on too much. I think that balance is most critical. Plus, I need to support my family in a way that is not leaving me scared that we won't have enough.

Coach: Is the topic about balance or self-employment vs. job?

Coachee: Balance. It is easier to find the balance with a job, however, it will be more rewarding to do self-employment and find balance there. I am in-between engagements. I want to find the balance. I got a job offer, but I need more information. What do I listen to inside me to make the decision?

Coach: What would you like to get out of our meeting today?

Coachee: I want to get as clear as I can on my inner guides. Safety and security is part of balance. Part of the choice of self-employment is to be open to options and pursue passion. I am off track again....but I want to find an inner guide. I am going in circles. I am trying to listen to the right voices.

There are lots of things I am paying attention to. I need to make a mindful choice to have the freedom.

Coach: I wonder if what I am hearing is what is going on in your head? I am hearing a lot of stuff. What do you need to focus on?

Coachee: You are right. I am swirling. I am spinning. I don't even have the information, there are lots of factors. It is about figuring out what I listen to. I have not done enough mindfulness. Sitting and meditating helps a lot to get more clear.

Coach: Is the focus on yesterday's job offer or just having criteria for the inner guide?

Coachee: The inner guide. I need to get clear on what I am listening to. I need to decide about employment.

Coach: What does that mean for you? Is it a checklist, a feeling…what do you look for as your inner guide?

Coachee: Part of my problem is that my gut is powerful in opposition. There are two parts of my gut. I am trying to connect head and heart. They are overactive and they fight with each other. I need clarity.

Coach: I wonder if it is hard for your gut to give a clear signal, because there is so much going on in your head?

Coachee: I have not even made my business vision. There are pros and cons for different jobs. There is a whole long list of things that pull me, and I need to decide on what is most important.

Coach: That is a good question – what is most important?

Coachee: I need to write down every little voice in my head and ask what is most important. This and this and this….there are all these different factors.

Coach: What if it was not so hard? What if there were only a couple of things that are most important?

Coachee: Maybe if I start by making a detailed list…

Coach: (stops the coachee from going down that route) What if you bypass the list and just ask yourself what is most important?

Coachee: Earning a good living and freedom to work at home.

Coach: How is it to be clear on that?

Coachee: Calmer.

Coach: With that calmness and clarity, how are you feeling about your inner guide?

Coachee: So much clearer. I can now evaluate yesterday's offer and future offers based on what is important.

Coach: How is that?

Coachee: So much calmer and easier. My head is not swirling anymore.

Coach: What are your next steps?

Coachee: I will think about yesterday's offer in light of what is important and make a decision about it.

Coach: What are you taking away from today's meeting that will help you move forward with clarity?

Coachee: Keeping things simple and focusing on what is important.

....

"

SUMMARY

- If you attempt to create awareness without first creating safety, trust and rapport, you may only achieve a superficial outcome with your coachee.
- Awareness is essential in change and transformation work. If the coachee is not aware that a change is required, then there will not be the intention or the motivation to make a change.
- The coach does not need to understand the coachee's issue. Rather, the coach's job is to help the coachee gain clarity.
- It is important to clearly identify the topic to be resolved or clarified as well as the desired outcome of the meeting. This allows the coach and coachee to have a way to measure the success of the meeting.
- Coaches use active listening techniques such as mirroring and paraphrasing to help their coachees be more clear and precise in their messages to others and themselves.
- Mirroring is repeating back the coachee's words so she hears her own words and has the opportunity to clarify them.
- Paraphrasing is summarizing the coachee's message, sometimes with new words, but with the intention of maintaining the original message.

Chapter 6 - Resources

Have you noticed that when people are upset or overwhelmed, they have a hard time coming up with solutions to their problems? All they can think of is the problem. In addition, even if the coachee is calm but still in a problematic headspace, she often can't imagine what is possible. One of the biggest lessons I learned as a coach was the concept of leading the coachee to a positive frame of mind before discussing new possibilities.

The Resource Stage

In the resources step, you help your coachee to identify and develop the resource(s) that she needs to resolve the issue or achieve the result she wants. In this step, you provide a risk-free zone in which she can brainstorm and test out creative solutions. You encourage her to consider possibilities that stretch her limits.

FOCUS ON STRENGTHS, NOT WEAKNESSES

I was born to be a project manager. I don't just enjoy this role; I actually can't help taking it on when I work with others. Planning, organizing, writing, strategizing — these tasks just come automatically to me.

I am **not** a natural sales person. Although I could invest time and energy to become passably good at the sales process, I have chosen instead to partner with someone who **is** a natural sales person. My partner is grateful for my organizational skills, and I am grateful for his masterful sales skills.

Sometimes we are taught to focus on improving our weaknesses rather than developing our strengths. I believe that this is a recipe for mediocrity. In *Now, Manage Your Strengths*[6], the authors take an entirely different approach. They recommend that we celebrate our strengths, and accept and learn to manage our flaws. In this manner, we can become well-rounded by addressing our shortfalls, but more importantly, we identify and grow our strengths.

When you focus only on developing your coachee's weaknesses, you may demoralize her, and your coaching work will yield marginal gains. For long term growth, allow your coachee the opportunity to develop her strengths to their full potential rather than focusing only on her weaknesses.

"You can do anything you put your heart, mind and soul into. Far more than you can imagine. Be fearless. Do it."
LL Cool J

Celebrate and grow your strengths. Accept and learn to manage your weaknesses.

---

6   Buckingham, M., & Clifton, PhD, D. O. (2001). Now, Manage Your Strengths. New York, NY: Simon & Schuster Inc.

LEADING YOUR COACHEE TO A POSITIVE STATE

Your coachee needs to be in a coachable state before she can identify new possibilities. Non-resourceful states such as feeling overwhelmed, being distracted, concerned with other people's opinions or unfocused, having conflicting values or limiting beliefs, and other negative emotions get in the way of your coachee's conscious connection to her inner wealth of resourcefulness.

Change in Physiology

One of the simplest ways to lead your coachee to a positive resource state is through a change in physiology. You can ask your coachee to:

- Stand up
- Look up
- Stretch
- Take some deep breaths
- Do some other physical movement that generates energy and strength or offers a new physical perspective

❝ A COACHING CONVERSATION (CHANGE IN PHYSIOLOGY)

.....

Coach: What resources do you need?

Coachee: I don't know. I just can't see the possibilities.

Coach: Try standing over here. (points)

Coachee: (moves to the new location)

Coach: Take a few deep breaths from there.

Coachee: (breathes)

Coach: From this perspective, what do you see about the resources that you need to achieve your goal?

Coachee: It looks different now. I definitely need confidence and clarity. ❞

....

Visualizations

You can also lead your coachee to a more positive state through the use of visualizations. You ask your coachee what resources (e.g. confidence or calmness) would benefit her right now, then help her remember a time in the past when she experienced those resources — even in an unrelated context.

Once the coachee is feeling more positive, she will then be open to exploring the full range of possibilities open to her.

A COACHING CONVERSATION (CHANGING STATE USING A VISUALIZATION)

.....

Coach: If you could fast-forward to the end of the successful conversation, what would you see?

Coachee: What a relief. It is to good to have the conversation over with. I can't believe I waited so long.

Coach: Looking back at the conversation, what resources did you have that made it successful?

Coachee: I was clear on what I needed to say. I was calm. I told him that, regardless of the outcome, I wanted us to stay friends and keep things respectful.

Coach: Calm, clear and respectful.

Coachee: Yes, that is what I need.

Coach: Can you remember a time when you felt calm?

Coachee: (pause) Yes, I was really calm when my daughter was talking about moving out of our house when she was only 16 years old.

Coach: Tell me more about that time.

Coachee: I did not want her to move out, but I knew that I could not force her to stay. I meditated every day and prayed for calmness and clarity.

Coach: So you had both, calmness and clarity?

Coachee: Yes.

"Take your time and let the conversation unfold. Ask each question without being compelled to get an instant answer that will end all exploration of the issue or challenge at hand."
John Sweetnam

Coach: Go into that feeling and remember what it was like.

Coachee: (long pause) Okay.

Coach: Can you remember a time when you were respectful of others?

Coachee: That same situation. I treated her respectfully. By staying calm, clear and respectful, she eventually came around and decided to stay home.

Coach: Go into that feeling. Remember what it was like to be calm, clear and respectful. She eventually came around.

Coachee: (pause) Yes, I can do that. I need to meditate every day, calm myself before the conversation, be respectful. It will all work out.

Coach: It will all work out. (pause) How do you feel now about the conversation?

Coachee: Really good. I can do this. I will do it.

....

> **99**

EXERCISE: POSITIVE RESOURCE STATES

The next time you are having a conversation with someone who is complaining or can't come up with possibilities, ask her if she is willing to see her situation from a different perspective. If she is willing, ask her:

1. What she would like to focus on
2. What her desired outcome is
3. What resources she needs to achieve that outcome

Then help her recall a time when she had those resources. When she is in a positive state, ask her how she feels about the topic.

REFLECTION

What impact did this exercise have on your coachee?

ASKING POWERFUL QUESTIONS

At each meeting, the coach asks open-ended, evocative questions to help the coachee identify and work through a specific topic with the aim of moving the coachee toward her overall goals. The questions are designed to challenge, clarify, and provoke new insights and lessons.

It is important to phrase questions precisely and in a manner that does not lead your coachee to the outcome that *you* want. Conversations should not become interrogations nor should they be judgmental. The coach simply guides the coachee towards the solution in a non-confrontational manner.

Powerful questions are used to get coachees to ask themselves things that they are avoiding or have not yet thought of asking. Don't be surprised if your questions cause your coachee to pause and think.

Sometimes questions are uncomfortable for both the coach and the coachee. Ask them anyhow.

When asking questions, slow down, listen to what the coachee has said, consider where you are in the CARA process, then pose a question to move the coachee towards action or clarity. There is no need to rush. On the contrary — it can be beneficial to the coachee if you slow down the process so she has time to reflect.

When it comes to questions, short is best. If you find yourself repeatedly paraphrasing for your client or speaking in long or complex sentences, ask yourself why you are speaking so much. It is very effective if you ask your *coachee* to summarize where she is at.

If you get flustered, stop, breathe, refocus and pose a simple question that will move your coachee towards her desired outcome.

WAIT: **W**hy **A**m **I T**alking?

Effective Questions in Coaching

The purpose of the dialogue, facilitated by asking questions, is to:

- Raise the coachee's self-awareness
- Invite responses that encourage the coachee to tell herself the truth
- Go beyond asking for information by asking for discovery
- Encourage the coachee to take responsibility for herself
- Keep the coachee focused on her topic, while being open to re-negotiation of the agreement
- Lead to learning for your coachee
- Address your coachee's needs

Tip: Powerful Questions:

- Are short
- Are open-ended
- Are solution-focused
- Follow a natural progression that moves the coachee towards the desired outcome
- Result in insights and greater clarity
- Usually do not include the word "I"

Bridge Words and Fillers

By definition, a bridge offers a pathway over an empty space or an obstacle. A bridge also connects two things. In conversations, bridge words like "so", and "hmmm" serve the same purpose — to help the coachee connect to a new insight that may be linked to the earlier idea. In addition, because some people process at a deeper level, bridge words can help them to make links that they might otherwise have missed.

Fillers are words like "um", "right" and "you know" that are inserted in the place of pauses at the beginning of sentences, at the end of sentences or when the speaker has lost her train of thought. They fill a gap and take up empty space, but they rarely add value. They can also be very distracting for the listener. Filler words dilute the message and make the speaker look disorganized and nervous.

Pauses, on the other hand, are tremendously beneficial for the coachee because they allow her to ponder the last question or simply have space to integrate new information. In many cases, pauses provide more value than an additional question.

Bridge Words	Filler Words
So …	Um…
And …	Right?
Mmm hmmm…	You know?
Yes…	Ok?
Go on…	

"Effective dialogue requires emotional safety for all participants; there must be no negative outcomes for expressing a point of view honestly and candidly."
Thomas Crane

Pauses

Pauses are a natural part of speech, not unwanted interruptions. They allow the coach and coachee to breathe, think and process information. Short pauses are used to separate thoughts, while longer pauses are used to get the audience to reflect on what was said. Pauses also indicate when it is the other person's turn to speak.

While your coachee's initial response to a question may be reactionary or superficial, allowing her the time to go inward helps her gain deeper insight. Many people think and talk very quickly and only scratch the surface of their thoughts and emotions. Pauses slow down the conversation and allow coachees to gain greater insights into themselves. A well-timed pause at the right time can be the turning point in a coaching meeting and can create an "aha" moment.

Stay Objective

Stay calm and listen without getting caught in the story. You don't need to fix anything. You just need to ask the right questions.

One of the basic premises of coaching is that the coachee already has the answer—you just need to help her uncover it. As coach, you can create a codependency if you provide solutions. Coaching is about meeting the coachee's needs—not yours. Resist the urge to just "give the answers." Your suggestion might be right for you, but not for your coachee. You may even take away her motivation by giving her the answer.

Your coachee already possesses or has access to the resources necessary to resolve her issues. Let her know that you believe that she is creative, resourceful and whole. Your responsibility is to help *her* to uncover and develop these skills and resources.

Your Client is in Charge and Sets the Pace

Your client chooses where to focus her efforts and decides the pace at which she makes changes. Your job is to find the balance between challenging and supporting, while keeping in mind that resistance to change is natural and often precedes deep change. If you notice resistance, confirm agreement with your client to continue. You can ask:

- Are you ready to solve this now?
- What are you gaining by holding onto this?
- Where else in your life is this surfacing?
- Is this the right time to address this?
- Is it safe to address this today?

DESCRIPTIVE VS. CREATIVE QUESTIONS

Both descriptive and creative language are helpful in forming coaching questions, but for different reasons. You use descriptive questions when you want the coachee to be more specific, grounded and concrete. You use creative questions when you want the coachee to be expansive and think outside the box.

Descriptive Questions

The purpose of descriptive questions is to describe, clarify and gather facts. You use descriptive questions when you want to increase comprehension of a situation or to reinforce a certain feeling or belief. Descriptive questions help your coachee to appreciate her situation in more depth, thereby creating greater understanding.

Descriptive questions can help your coachees get to a deeper level of feeling and thinking. It is in this space that coachees can create significant shifts.

If used at the wrong time, descriptive questions can cause your coachee to become too analytical or too focused to be open to new possibilities. When this happens, your coachee may become unresourceful or disempowered.

Examples of Descriptive Questions

- What did you notice about...?
- What did you observe about..?
- How would you know...?
- What is an example of...?
- How does that relate to...?
- Can you describe....?
- What specifically about that....?
- What is different about that vs. _____ ?

66 A COACHING CONVERSATION

Notice the use of descriptive questions to clarify the meeting agreement.

Coach: What would you like to focus on today?
Coachee: It has been a horrible week. My wife and I had a terrible fight. I am so tired of this. I have been thinking of a separation. I don't know what to do. I feel guilty just thinking about it.
Coach: Sounds like a stressful week. I heard a few things. What would you like to focus on today?
Coachee: I need to have a real conversation with her. No shouting. She is so angry.
Coach: What is that like...a real conversation?
....

Creative Questions

The purpose of creative questions is to imagine new possibilities. It is from this perspective that coaches can catalyze change and transformation in their coachees.

Creative questions are expansive and allow the coachee to be in a space where anything is possible. She may not know how to get

> *"Each of us needs periods in which our minds can focus inwardly. Solitude is an essential experience for the mind to organize its own processes and create an internal state of resonance. "*
>
> **Dan J. Siegel**

there, but the options are *out in front*. If used at the wrong time, creative questions can confuse or overwhelm the coachee.

Examples of Creative Questions

- What does that reveal to you?
- What is possible?
- What if you didn't know….?
- What is underneath that?
- What did you discover about…?
- What does that connect you to?
- Who else will you be then?
- What possibilities does that open you to?
- What does that allow?
- If anything were possible?
- If you could have 3 wishes, what would they be?

❝ A COACHING CONVERSATION

Notice how creative questions are used to stimulate new thinking.

….
Coach: What other possibilities are there?
Coachee: I could get babysitter to watch the kids so we are not distracted or tired.
Coach: What does that allow?
Coachee: Sometimes when we talk after the kids go to bed, it is just too late. This would take away the distractions and let the conversation be the focus.
Coach: If you could have three wishes, what would they be?
Coachee: (tears) To actually have a real conversation with my wife again. To see my wife look at me like she used to. To have a peaceful home again.
Coach: What will that allow?
Coachee: It would be so much easier to deal with things.   ❞
….

Tips for Asking Questions

- If you have a talkative coachee, frame your questions with time boundaries (e.g. suggest that your client respond in a few sentences or a minute or two).
- Elicit a metaphor related to the original issue and get your coachee to make the links.
- Watch for energy shifts.
- Make your questions short.
- Leave time for your coachee to integrate the question — even if it seems uncomfortable.
- Avoid questions beginning with "why" as it brings the client to explaining and defending, rather than exploring.
- As coaches, we love to help people. Remember, we are a resource to help coachees connect with their *own* resources. Resist the temptation to give the coachee the answers. Instead, use questions so she can come up with her own answers.

EXERCISE

Over the next few days experiment with descriptive and creative questions. Ask yourself:

- "Is it my intention to clarify details or to stimulate innovation?"
- "Is the coachee overwhelmed by all of the possibilities?" If yes, then use a descriptive question to sum up where she is now.
- "Is the coachee explaining instead of exploring?" If yes, add a creative question to create new perspectives

When to Use Descriptive vs. Creative Questions

Descriptive questions are used when the coach wants the coachee
to be specific such as when:

- Clarifying where the coachee is at now
- Clarifying past events
- Making links between two events
- Making links to metaphors
- Eliciting the meeting agreement
- Discussing past successes
- Asking the coachee to commit to actions
- Asking for takeaways from the meeting

Creative questions are used when the coach wants the coachee to
think beyond her current boundaries such as when:

- Generating new resource possibilities
- Developing new action possibilities
- Eliciting next steps
- Imagining stretch goals

QUESTIONS TO GENERATE POSSIBILITIES

- What do you need?
- How do you need to be?
- Who will you be?
- What resources are available to you?
- What resources do you need?
- What is important?
- What is really important?
- What is the biggest challenge you have?
- How do you know that?
- How could you simplify that?
- If you had a choice, what would you do?
- What is your biggest fear about that?

- What question do you need to ask yourself?
- Is this a need or a want?
- What resource do you need in order to resolve this issue?
- What does your ideal life look like?
- What gets you out of bed each day?
- Do you recall a time when you had that resource?
- What was it like when you fully used that resource?
- If you had that resource in place, how would the issue look/feel now?
- How would having that resource help resolve the issue?
- How would you be different if you had that resource in place?

" A COACHING CONVERSATION

Notice the use of pauses and descriptive vs. creative questions.
Notice how few words are used in the questions and how the
coachee's words are incorporated into the coach's language.
Finally, notice how the client sets the pace.

Coach: What do you want to focus on today?

*Coachee: When I am in conversations, whether romantic or at work, when
things are expressed to me and I am not feeling resourceful, I shut down
instead of drawing on my skills and resources. I want to have courageous
conversations.*

Coach: Where would you like to start?

Coachee: I would like to be **in** *those moments, to draw on my resources, be
peaceful, express what I need, ask for clarification, be resourceful so I can
have the conversation. The more I shut down and delay, things are not
working for me.*

Coach: What is the best way to explore this?

*Coachee: A couple of things come to me. One: I wonder if this stems from the
positive reinforcement I got when I was a kid for being content and quiet and
just happy. I remember once when the family was in the car, my Dad said,
'Look how quiet and content she is. And happy.' I wonder how much power
that holds. I am always trying to be happy and not get in conflicts. Two: I get
out of sorts, and I lose my anchor to my resources. Maybe addressing both of
those.*

Coach: What are your beliefs about experiencing these emotions?

*Coachee: It is important, emotions should not be shut down. I want to be
able to express them so the little things don't turn into big things.*

Coach: What do you think the issue is?

*Coachee: I want to stay resourceful when I feel a negative emotion. It is ok
for me to feel the emotion, and necessary, but what I want to change is being
resourceful so I can talk it through as opposed to shutting down.*

Coach: What is resourceful for you?

Coachee: In general, resourceful is being able to express, talk, listen and ask questions even though I might be sad or even angry. I don't want to shut down.

Coach: (pause) What might be going on underneath?

Coachee: A fear of not being liked. Wanting to be accepted.

Coach: When you hear yourself say those things, what comes up?

Coachee: I am laughing at myself because I thought I had addressed these things. I guess it is another layer.

Coach: Is it time to look at this layer?

Coachee: Yes.

Coach: Would you be willing to sink into that feeling, that part inside of you that is feeling that?

Coachee: Yes.

Coach: Where is that residing in you?

Coachee: The bottom of my stomach.

Coach: How is that feeling?

Coachee: Heavily constricted.

Coach: Can you put your attention down inside there?

Coachee: Yes.

Coach: Let me know when you have settled in there.

Coachee: (pause) Okay.

Coach: Just breathe and relax in there to experience the feelings. What is coming up for you?

Coachee: A couple of memories of getting positive reinforcement for being happy and content.

Coach: How does that positive reinforcement relate to the constricted feeling?

Coachee: The tightening releases and goes away.

Coach: Why do you think that memory is coming up and how does it relate to what is going on today?

Coachee: The two are linked. I am looking for approval.

Coach: What would be even better?

Coachee: Acceptance of myself that I am okay. I am great the way I am. To love myself.

Coach: Knowing that you are great, just the way you are and you love yourself, what is possible now?

Coachee: I can express myself, I can communicate. I can even ask questions. That is a small step versus not saying anything.

Coach: If you could have anything you want, what would it be?

Coachee: That is a big question! To be anchored in my peaceful, loving space of myself and others, and to simply speak, ask a question or tell the person what I am feeling, speak freely.

Coach: What is the best way to get anchored in your peaceful, loving space?

Coachee: To actually do it. To bring up different memories of when I had that feeling.

Coach: I know you are a feeling person. Would you like to go inside and find those memories and notice where they are?

Coachee: The first one is when my daughter was born and she was put on my chest.

Coach: Where does that come up in your body?

Coachee: Through my chest.

Coach: Do you want to stay there for a bit or look for others?

Coachee: (very long pause) This is good.

Coach: If I repeat back 'peaceful loving space of self and others', does that bring up anything?

Coachee: When I stand up, I go inside, I am connected to the energy that I am feeling. (Coachee stands)

Coach: (pause) How are you feeling now?

Coachee: Very peaceful and solid, comfortable, resourceful, loving, connected, I can feel the energy through me.

Coach: When you are in this place, what is possible now?

Coachee: Everything.

Coach: How do those conversations look or feel now?

Coachee: They feel good, they are opportunities for open communications. I can say how I feel.

Coach: What do you notice that is different from how you were approaching those conversations before?

Coachee: Now I am approaching it from a positive attitude and approach.

*Coach: Are there next steps or is it just **being** different?*

Coachee: Being different.

Coach: How would you sum up what is different?

Coachee: The conversations are an opportunity for open communications. It is my own attitude that is going to drive the situation.

Coach: If you can go back to that place at the bottom of your stomach, knowing that conversations are opportunities, how is it feeling now?

Coachee: Great. I feel great. I feel connected to my body, to my center.

Coach: Do you have any last points to summarize where you are now or where you are going?

Coachee: My attitude and approach is key. I need to focus on the opportunities. On what I want, not what I don't want. That is the bottom line.

Coach: Thank you.

"

Chapter 7 - Action

"Vision without action is daydream. Action without vision is nightmare."
Japanese Proverb

The action stage of the conversation creates the forward momentum of the coaching relationship. In this stage, the coachee sums up the new ideas, chooses those that will best support her goals and makes a plan for implementation. This is also the time to reinforce the key lessons from the discussion.

I am very task focused, so I never have trouble introducing the action stage of the conversation — that has always been my favorite part. What I failed to realize, however, was that when you take the time to connect, create an awareness of the topic and fully explore the options, you require very little time and effort to negotiate action steps and accountability because they flow naturally out of the conversation. The coachee already knows what to do at this point in the conversation and it is often just a matter of choosing and summarizing the most important next steps.

If you find that generating the next step is taking too much effort, backtrack to one of the previous stages. It is possible that the original topic is no longer relevant, you may have lost rapport or perhaps you did not explore the possibilities fully enough.

At times the coachee is so pumped about her next steps that we can barely wrap up the meeting. This occurs when the topic is very important to her, she is highly motivated to implement changes and she feels capable of taking the next steps (even if there is a challenge involved).

Action

Prior to the completion of a coaching meeting, you help the coachee identify and choose the next steps that will reinforce what she has learned during the meeting and move her towards her desired outcome. The intention is to explore and select tangible action steps that can be implemented in the immediate future. Although the action possibilities are originated by the coachee, the coach can also make requests that challenge the coachee to take risks that will provide growth opportunities.

Action steps must be manageable for where your coachee is now, not where you think she should be. If she is having difficulty committing to or completing her action step, then most likely:

- The action step does not fit with her values
- She does not yet have the skills or resources to complete this step
- She has committed to more than she can handle

If it is important enough, and there is sufficient motivation to create change, the action steps will be compelling. The steps may not always be easy, but there will be enough momentum to push the coachee forward. If your coachee is having trouble with this step, take her back to generate deeper awareness or to build a positive resource state.

At your next meeting, ask your coachee to update you on her planned action steps. The intention of this is not to embarrass her if the actions were not completed, but rather to celebrate successes or to explore the reasons why the steps were not taken. In either case, this review provides opportunities for insights and to reinforce success. To generate possibilities for action, ask:

- What changes can you make moving forward?
- What if nothing changed?
- What is possible?
- Is there another way?
- What is in the way?
- What would need to change in order for this to happen?
- What is the next smallest step you will take?
- Is there anything else you would like to commit to right now?
- How committed are you?
- Do you have the resources to do this?
- What support do you have in place?
- How will you know if that has been successful?

"There are two mistakes one can make along the road to truth: not going all the way, and not starting."
Buddha

ACCOUNTABILITY

Many coaches end the coaching meeting after the coachee defines her next steps, but do not fully complete the session by clarifying accountability. Accountability includes:

- Having a clear meeting agreement, and reviewing the agreement at the end of the meeting to ensure that the coachee met her desired goals
- Having clear action steps to be completed following the coaching meeting
- Uncovering the motivations and benefits of following through on the action steps
- Helping the coachee to determine who, if anyone, will be on her accountability team and how she wants to be held

accountable
- Reviewing action items from the previous meeting, reinforcing successes and lessons from unmet action items

THE ACCOUNTABILITY SEQUENCE

Accountability is an essential, but sometimes neglected, part of coaching. Without accountability, the conversation lacks forward momentum and follow up. The following steps will help you to fully negotiate and follow through on accountability.

1. Negotiate the Meeting Agreement

The coach guides the coachee to commit to a meeting agreement.

- **Topic**: What the coachee wants to focus on
- **Outcome**: What the coachee wants to get out of the conversation

❝ A COACHING CONVERSATION

Coach: What would you like to focus on today?
Coachee: I am pretty stressed. I need to set and enforce boundaries with my son **(The Topic)**
Coach: How will you know that this has been a successful meeting?
Coachee: I will be clear on my boundaries, I will know how to communicate them and what to do when they are crossed.
Coach: I have heard three topics. Which is the most important to focus on first?
Coachee: I would like to start by getting clear on my boundaries. If we have time, we can talk about the other two. **(Clarifying the topic)**
Coach: What will you have at the end of the meeting that you don't have now?
Coachee: I don't know.
Coach: What is happening now that is causing this to be important?

Coachee: My son is violating our house rules. They are simple rules, but we can't seem to agree on them. It is causing a lot of tension in the house. (**Motivation**)

Coach: What would you like to have instead?

Coachee: I want to talk through our house rules and understand what our bottom line is. I want to know at what point enough is enough. (**Outcome**)

Coach: How will you know that you have that?

Coachee: (pause) The rules will be few and easily understood. I will know the consequences associated with each of them and how to communicate them.

Coach: Is that what you would like to get out of the meeting?

Coachee: Yes.

Coach: How will that feel?

Coachee: Relief. Clarity.

Coach: How are you feeling right now?

Coachee: Stressed. Uncertain. (**Measurement now**)

Coach: At the end of the meeting, how will you know that you have relief and clarity?

Coachee: (pause) I will feel it in my chest and my body will feel strong.

(**Measurement at the end of the conversation**)

....

2. Action Steps and Accountability

After exploring the topic and possibilities, the coachee clearly identifies her next steps (actions). These steps should be concisely summarized, measurable, time-bound and relevant to moving forward on the meeting agreement.

 ....

Coach: What are your next steps?

Coachee: My husband and I will meet with our son to communicate our boundaries.

Coach: When?

Coachee: I think we will wait until this weekend.

Coach: You think?

Coachee: We **will** *meet on the weekend when there is more time to have the discussion.*

Coach: Is there anything you need to do in advance to create the conditions for a successful discussion?

Coachee: We need to have some ground rules about language and respect.

Coach: How will you prepare for that?

Coachee: I think we just need to, one: set up a time for the conversation, two: discuss the ground rules up front and what we will do if he gets angry, and three: have the conversation.

Coach: How does that sound?

Coachee: Good. We can do this. We need to do this.

....

In this step, you also ask the coachee what she needs to keep her accountable to her commitment and how she would like you to follow up with her. Typically, the coach checks in with the coachee at the next meeting, but at times the coachee will ask if she can send the coach a follow-up email when the next steps are completed. In either case, the coachee decides how she wants to demonstrate her accountability.

 ...

Coach: How will you stay accountable to your commitment?

Coachee: I will talk to my husband tonight to prepare. We will make sure we are calm before the conversation. We need to have this conversation.

....

3. Accountability to the Agreement

Sometimes the options and possibilities sound good until it is time to implement them. The discussion of accountability is intended to create a way to keep the coachee "answerable" to her commitment. It also ensures that the coachee has sufficient internal motivation to complete the next steps. The coach's role is to test the coachee's readiness and help her overcome obstacles to success. It can be helpful to create a future vision of this success.

> ....
>
> *Coach: When I speak to you next week, what will you say to me?*
> *Coachee: That we met with our son on the weekend. We were calm. We set ground rules. The conversation went smoothly, and we all agreed on the rules.*
> *Coach: How are you feeling now about relief and clarity?*
> *Coachee: Good. Really good. I am clear on what we need to do, and relieved that we will get this conversation out of the way.*
>
> ....

Coaches are not attached to the coachee's outcome. The intention of accountability is not to embarrass the coachee if she does not complete her next steps, but rather to hold a mirror up to her to reflect her actions. Regardless of the outcome, the coach simply accepts that the coachee has done her best given the circumstances.

The outcome is not a reflection of the coach; it is simply a reflection of where the coachee is in her forward movement.

The coach is also responsible for keeping the coachee aware of and accountable to her long-term goals.

> ....
>
> *Coach: How does this fit in with your long-term goals?*
> *Coachee: I need to get this sorted out. It is affecting my sleep and my ability to work.*
>
> ....

4. Wrap-Up

Before closing the meeting, ask the coachee what she has learned that will help her to move forward with her topic. This reinforces the awareness that was generated during the coaching meeting and helps to solidify why her next steps are important to generate forward movement.

 ....

Coach: What is the most important thing you are taking away from today's meeting?

Coachee: These types of conversations need to happen. If we stay calm and have ground rules, we can do it while maintaining our relationship.

5. Follow-Up

At your next meeting, ask your coachee to update you on the actions that she committed to. If, for example, the coachee has not had the conversation that she committed to, a coachable moment is there to be seized. There is value in exploring the explanation, as this perspective offers up the possibility of uncovering a blind spot in the coachee. Be sure to approach the discussion from a place of compassion, with the intent to move the coachee forward.

"Prancing around in our comfort zones is great for stroking the ego but not so much for growing and evolving. Stumble, fail, fall flat on your face — all proof that you're doing something right."
Rebekah "Bex" Borucki

66 A COACHING CONVERSATION

Notice the negotiation of the agreement and how the coach closes the loop to ensure accountability to the agreement.

Coach: How would you like to use our time together today?

Coachee: I would like to talk about my future business development as a coach. I can give you a bit of a background and what I am interested in. I retired from leadership work in healthcare a year ago. In the past few years, I transitioned into taking coaching courses for my retirement so I would be able to retire from executive leadership work and do leadership coaching with leaders and their teams. And that has happened. I am starting to think about what I want to do with my coaching business. I am really enjoying retirement. I want to work, but I want to really enjoy my retirement and travel. The thing I want to talk about is that I don't want to set the world on fire. My purpose is to enjoy both retirement and stay focused on coaching at a modest level. I don't know how I will do that. I don't have the desire for a major marketing campaign.

Coach: You are enjoying your free time in retirement, the time to travel and at the same time, you feel compelled to coach. What I am hearing is that you want a moderate level of coaching.

Coachee: Right. I love it when I am doing it. But I don't want to push hard to get mega-clients and big contracts.

Coach: What would you like to have at the end of our meeting?

Coachee: The only kind of work I have ever known has been 10-12 hour days, really pushing hard. Where I am wanting the clarity is that I don't want to be fully retired, but I don't want to feel like I am pushing hard with work. Maybe I am trying to give myself permission to not hit it hard. To just flow. Go with the flow as opposed to feeling like something I have to be doing.

Coach: You want permission?

Coachee: Yes. I have some anxiety that if I relax too much I won't get the clients that I want, but if I get too enmeshed in work, I can't relax the way I want to. I feel that I have to make something happen, but I am not sure if that is true. Maybe I can relax into this. I don't want a lot of clients but I want clients who will help me stretch.

Coach: You want to grow in your practice.

Coachee: Yes. Professional skills development.

Coach: How will you feel when you are flowing?

Coachee: Relaxed. Fluid. Ready to go with the flow.

Coach: What is the best question you can ask yourself?

Coachee: (Long pause) How can I build trust and confidence in myself as it relates to the flow of my coaching business?

Coach: How can I build trust and confidence in myself as it relates to the flow of my coaching business?

Coachee: Yes. That is it. Wow – that is really helpful. It is about trusting myself and my skills and who I am as a coach and as a person.

Coach: What kind of trust is that trust?

Coachee: (Long pause) Relaxing into possibilities and the flow, not overthinking it, being the best I can be. I recently received a nice contract. It is marvelous. It happened by networking. It is because of who I am and the people that I know. I didn't do anything special except to be who I am.

Coach: Earlier you said 'I don't want to work too hard.' Did you work too hard?

Coachee: (laughs) It is no work at all to be who I am. I want to be able to flow with this, network, put myself out there, be myself and let it happen. I don't want to start a major marketing campaign….and I want to be a continuous learner. I am also going to update my website. To make it reflect who I am as a coach and how I want to represent myself.

Coach: As you think about these things, networking, continuing education, website, how do you feel?

Coachee: Really good. It is really helpful. It was good to talk through this

Coach: How is the flow now?

Coachee: Great. I am in the flow. Relaxed.

Coach: It seems exciting rather than a lot of work.

Coachee: Yes, easy when you are yourself and flowing.

Coach: What are your next steps?

Coachee: Call the web designer and otherwise, just be me, continue to network, and let it happen. Go with the flow.

Coach: What are you taking way from our conversation?

Coachee: This does not need to be hard work. I can be me and let it flow. I feel more relaxed instead of anxious.

Coach: How will you stay in the flow, or get back to it, if you start working too hard?

Coachee: I will remember how easy it was to get the contract just by being myself.

Coach: How will you remember that?

Coachee: It is already embedded.

"

SUMMARY

"At some point you must stop asking questions and start taking action."
Anthony Robbins

- The coaching meeting is not complete until the coachee has fully committed to her action plan and has defined how she will be accountable for her actions.
- Accountability is not an afterthought to be squeezed in during the last couple of minutes of the coaching meeting.
- If the coachee is having trouble defining or committing to actions, backtrack to the connection, awareness or resources stages.

Part 3

Become a Coach Leader

CHAPTER 8 - MASTERFUL PERFORMANCE FEEDBACK

Giving masterful feedback is an essential coach leader skill that creates stronger teams and relationships. When a leader does not have these skills, it can derail relationships and cause distrust. Providing feedback reinforces excellence, lets others know exactly what you appreciate and acknowledge about them and, when used constructively, helps someone or some situation to be different. It is used to help others become their best selves.

Becoming masterful at giving compassionate feedback will help you become a treasured leader, manager, parent, friend or co-worker.

Providing timely and useful performance feedback has become a cornerstone for me. After some experiences in my early twenties when I did not have the courage and skills to provide honest feedback, I became convinced of the benefits of early and frank discussions.

When engaging with others, I now pay close attention to my feelings, emotions and intuition. When something does not feel right to me, I have learned that it is beneficial to bring it up as soon as possible. It can be as simple as asking a co-worker:

Coach: You seem upset. Is everything ok?

For more substantial or repeat behaviors you might say:

Coach: Joy, I noticed at our last two meetings that you didn't contribute to the discussion. Can we take a moment to discuss this?

In the two previous examples, there may be absolutely nothing wrong; however, following up with the person gives her the opportunity to tell you what is on her mind before strong feelings build up. I have learned to trust my intuition and found that laying my thoughts on the table and stating my feelings can create more trust. At a minimum, it helps to clarify the situation.

Giving masterful performance feedback is an essential coach leader skill that creates stronger teams and relationships.

LACK OF FEEDBACK OR INAPPROPRIATE FEEDBACK

Without proper feedback, problems often get ignored until the person is shuffled off to the next manager, or the problem becomes unmanageable. In a work place, the person may be let go. Sometimes parents are unwilling or unable to provide feedback to their children in a way that is understandable and provides motivation for change. This cycle does not only affect the person with the problem; other employees or family members get frustrated and angry when the leader does not deal with problem behaviors. Sometimes the person with the problem is treated with kid gloves and is released from taking a full workload, or allowed to behave inappropriately.

Feedback is not only used for correcting problems. It is also used to acknowledge and reinforce excellence. This will be addressed more fully in Chapter 10 - Acknowledgment. If the feedback is careless or imprecise, it can have the opposite effect of what was intended. The recipient may feel that the person delivering the feedback was patronizing or did not truly appreciate the work. If the feedback is not specific, the recipient may not understand what behaviors were valued; this is a missed growth opportunity.

FEEDBACK IS NOT PRAISE

Performance feedback is delivered with the intention of acknowledging what is happening now (with concrete examples), reinforcing what is working well and developing a plan to improve areas that are not working well. Although direct language is used, the feedback is delivered in a manner such that the recipient has the opportunity to self-discover her weaknesses and co-create her own plan for improvement.

CONSTRUCTIVE CRITICISM

Most of us have experienced so-called *constructive criticism* at some point in our lives. This type of feedback can leave us feeling angry and judged. It may work temporarily in environments where the recipient can be bullied into making a change, but it will likely create long term resentment and underlying anger. When the recipient feels this way, it can be hard to get past the defensiveness to catalyze long term changes. Sometimes stubbornness will surface, and the feedback will be resisted entirely.

MASTERFUL PERFORMANCE FEEDBACK

The way that we give performance feedback is critical to the development or maintenance of the dynamics of a relationship. Some of us have been fortunate to receive masterful feedback from someone who cares deeply about us. Those who are masters at delivering feedback have developed the skill of offering feedback in areas that the recipient needs to improve, while ensuring that she does not feel judged or coerced into making changes. When this type of feedback is offered, the recipient has the opportunity to reinforce her strengths and explore her shortfalls with the aim of moving towards self-improvement.

Vague "atta boy" comments are not precise enough to highlight desired behaviors, constructive criticism does not reinforce excellence, and telling people what to do or change does not promote growth or learning. Masterful feedback, on the other hand, results in the coachee feeling like she is making a positive step forward in her career or life. With this style of feedback, the coachee is clear on where she stands with the coach leader, feels supported in her growth and develops a stronger bond with the coach leader.

TESTIMONIAL

"What works for me is when feedback is presented as facts…actual facts — no insinuated facts or third-party facts. I want to hear the real goods. When it is presented in a fashion that is compassionate and neutral….no angry, off-the-wall ranting (we have all been exposed to that at one time or another). I also like it when it is presented to me one-on-one, not in a crowd, and I want it in appropriate language."

Walt

PERMISSION TO GIVE FEEDBACK

As with any coaching conversation, you need permission to give feedback because it is possible that:

- The feedback is appreciated, but the recipient is busy or distracted at the moment.
- The recipient wants feedback, but does not want to receive it from you.
- The recipient is not open to feedback.

For feedback to be effective, you must respect the wishes of the recipient because she really does know what is best for her at any given time.

TESTIMONIAL

"During my performance review discussion, while we were still discussing some of my accomplishments, I received feedback that completely dismissed any good work that I had presented over the past two years. The feedback lacked context; it was presented from a 3ʳᵈ-party perspective, and was delivered in a very casual, vague and unproductive manner. When I asked for context or a specific example, it was clear that this was not only uncomfortable for the feedback provider, but the information was unavailable. In that moment, I stopped talking. I shut down. I didn't even want to talk about my other accomplishments, because in that moment, I felt that I had nothing else to offer."

Alison

"Today when I look back at some of the feedback I have received from supervisors in my previous jobs, I remember the feeling of being manipulated and cornered. Even areas where I felt good about my accomplishments were made to appear that it was not good enough. I distinctly remember feeling there was a hidden agenda to the feedback.

This left me with a feeling of low self-worth and self-esteem, and I remember leaving those meetings making plans to look for another job where I would be more appreciated.

But then on the other hand, I have also been fortunate to have received feedback from a supervisor that was uplifting, constructive and empowering.

When I reflect back on the two scenarios, I think that what made the difference was the genuine concern the latter had for me as an individual. I trusted the supervisor and therefore was open to the feedback as a development and learning opportunity. It was feedback from the heart with no hidden agendas — only a genuine commitment to work towards my betterment."

Ian

REFLECTION

Describe a time when you received masterful feedback from someone.

What beliefs did the observer have about you?

What values did the observer hold?

What techniques/methods did the observer use to give you feedback?

What else was present to make the experience beneficial?

"Requesting and receiving permission to give feedback is one of the most crucial steps in the transformational coaching process."
Thomas Crane

Constructive Feedback

There are times when you need to give feedback for disciplinary reasons because the recipient has made a mistake or behaved inappropriately. If you begin this type of feedback with the assumption that you know what is best for the other person, or that the other person is either deficient or has deliberately done something wrong, the meeting begins with a negative energy that will be difficult to overcome and the recipient will be on the defensive. Several of the "assumptions" that were discussed in **Part 2 - The CARA Process**, will help you to create an open forum for discussion. For the best possible outcome, assume that:

1. Every behavior has a positive intention.

Even though you may not understand why the person behaved the way she did, begin the conversation with the belief that she had a positive intention for her behavior and use questions to uncover that purpose. By understanding what motivates her, you can help her to achieve her goal in other ways.

2. There is no failure only feedback.

If you will be giving feedback regarding poor performance or to discipline someone, help her understand that feedback is simply a means to learning. Ensure that you highlight the work that she is doing well and don't wait until you have multiple behaviors to provide feedback on. People can generally only focus effectively on changing one or two things at a time.

3. Every behavior is useful in some context.

While the recipient's behavior may not have worked in the context for which you are providing feedback, it was likely effective in some other context. Don't ridicule her. Simply help her understand what behaviors you are looking for.

4. Everyone is always doing what they believe is right.

In her model of the world, the recipient believed that what she was doing was right. Take the time to understand her thinking and help her to understand what is appropriate in your setting.

5. The behavior or decision that an individual makes is the best choice available to her given the circumstances as she sees it.

Sometimes when we are under stress, it is hard to appreciate all of the possibilities available to us, and we make choices that we would not make under ideal circumstances. Take the time to understand what was going on for the recipient and help her to make better choices in the future.

PRINCIPLES FOR GIVING MASTERFUL FEEDBACK

Truth and Honesty

Although most people say that they want truth and honesty from others, the truth is much more digestible when served with care. If we give the recipient the benefit of the doubt and follow the appreciative inquiry approach of reinforcing what is working and building upon that, we create a supportive atmosphere where the recipient is in a positive frame of mind; this keeps the recipient open to receiving additional information. We do this by reinforcing what is already working well and by referring to a specific example of the behavior that we want to reinforce.[7]

Positive Intention

The recipient will feel your intention through your words, body language, and tone of voice. Approach feedback carefully and

---

7   Flaherty, J. (2005). Coaching: Evoking excellence in others. (p. 75). Jordan Hill, Oxford: Routledge.

with the goal of creating trust, openness and a positive outcome that supports the growth of the recipient.

> You must have a positive intention for the recipient of your information — otherwise it is simply criticism designed to make you feel *right* or more powerful.

STEPS TO GIVING MASTERFUL FEEDBACK USING THE CARA PROCESS

1. Connect:

Choose an appropriate time and setting for the feedback

Feedback should be given one-on-one in a private setting to preserve the dignity of the recipient and create safety. Additionally, it should be delivered at a time when both parties are free of distractions and have the time and energy to focus on the conversation.

2. Connect:

Build rapport

Take a moment to build rapport and connect with the recipient of the feedback before launching into the actual feedback.

3. Awareness:

Request permission to give constructive feedback and create an agreement regarding the purpose of the feedback

There are times when the recipient has no choice but to receive feedback, nor does she have a choice in who gives it to her; however, be aware that the recipient may not be in the appropriate state of mind to receive feedback at that moment.

Requesting permission to give constructive feedback demonstrates respect for the recipient and, when granted, opens the door to a conversation that can lead to deeper rapport and connection.

> *Coach: Mike, I would like to talk to you about what happened yesterday when you caught Steve behaving irresponsibly on the forklift. Is now a good time?*
> *Coachee: Rob is waiting for me to give him today's safety report, can I come to your office in 10 minutes?*
> *Coach: Of course.*
> *....*

4. Awareness:

Negotiate the agreement

Let the recipient know your positive intentions and why it is important to you, the recipient and the organization. Agree on what you would like to explore together and the desired outcome of the conversation (the meeting agreement).

> *Coach: Mike, can we take 10 minutes to talk about yesterday's incident and how you handled it?*
> *Coachee: I know that I shouldn't have used the language that I did. It won't happen again.*
> *Coach: I am glad to hear that you are ready to change your language. My intention today is not to just criticize what happened yesterday. Safety is important to our bottom line. We value you as our safety manager, and this has happened twice now. Can we spend a few minutes reviewing what happened, and what you can do differently in the future?*
> *Coachee: Yes.*

Coach: What outcome would you like from the conversation?
Coachee: I want you to know that I regret what I said, and I would like to be calmer the next time I deal with something like this.

.....

5. Awareness:

Acknowledge what is already working well

Let the recipient know, with specific and recent examples, what is already working well and why you value that behavior or result.

Coach: Before we get into what happened yesterday, I want to acknowledge some really positive things you are adding to the safety program. First, I was impressed when I watched your last safety talk, and you had enlisted the team members to research and present the daily topic. I think that they are paying attention much more than they used to. I also want to acknowledge the huge improvement in the safety paperwork.
Coachee: Thank you. I have lots more ideas that I want to implement, too.
Coach: I am glad to hear that.

....

6. Awareness:

Give examples

Give specific, recent examples of what you personally have observed — without judgment. Do not pass on third party stories. The examples should be relevant to your feedback. If there is a problem, don't wait until it is out of hand. Give the feedback as soon as possible with the aim of helping the recipient plan for and create the future she wants.

Coach: Mike, you know that I am a big fan of yours, and I know that our

safety program has improved a lot since you became our safety supervisor.
I am concerned, however, that twice now, when you disciplined team
members, you swore at them and spoke in a very rude manner. Can you tell
me what happened, and what you would like to do differently next time?
Coachee: I don't know what came over me. I saw him with an unbalanced
load and he almost hit the door frame, I just lost it. I wish I could take it back.
Coach: These things will likely come up from time to time. How would you
like to handle them in the future?
Coachee: I would like to be calm and respectful. I would like to have a
conversation like this. I want the guys to be comfortable asking me safety
questions and not think I am a total jerk.
....

7. Resources:

Identify ways for the recipient to achieve the new objective or result

With positive language, help the recipient identify the gaps (new resources, skills or behaviors that will be required to attain the new outcome).   Be clear on why this new outcome or result is desired and how it will help you, the recipient and the organization.

Ask learning questions to help the recipient explore how she can implement the new resources, skills or behaviors in a way that is meaningful to her.

 ....

Coach: Calm and respectful. Can you tell me more about what that would be like?
Coachee: I guess it's like disciplining children. You should never do it when you are angry. Next time, I need to stop the dangerous situation, make it safe, then take a couple of breaths before talking to the team member. I should never swear at someone. I just won't do it.
Coach: How does it affect your credibility when you swear?

Coachee: The one who looks bad is me.

Coach: How do you think the team member feels when you shout and swear?

Coachee: The person is probably so mad at me that he is not listening to what I am saying.

Coach: What does that tell you?

Coachee: I can never do that again. I will make the situation safe, breathe, tell the person what is unsafe. Next, I will talk to him the way you are talking to me. I will ask him what he needs to do differently.

Coach: How will the person react when you are calm and respectful?

Coachee: He will be calm enough to learn the lesson and will respect me for teaching him instead of berating him.

....

8. Action:

Next steps

Guide the recipient to identify action steps that will help her to acquire or implement the new resources, skills or behaviors.

" ....

Coach: What are your next steps to implement these new behaviors?

Coachee: I will be calm and respectful and help the person learn what he did wrong instead of make him feel stupid.

Coach: How will you remember to do that?

Coachee: I am going to start practicing right away on small things. I will remind myself to stay calm, breathe and speak respectfully.

....

9. Wrap-up:

Reinforce what was learned

Ask the recipient for takeaways, lessons or comments that reinforce the new behaviors.

❝ ....

Coach: What is the most important lesson you are taking from our conversation today?

Coachee: Treating team members disrespectfully has the opposite effect that I want. I will get a better outcome if I am calm and respectful. **❞**

GIVING FEEDBACK – IN A NUTSHELL

1. Choose an appropriate time and setting for the feedback
2. Build rapport
3. Acknowledge what is already working well
4. Request permission to give constructive feedback
5. Create an agreement
6. Give specific, and recent, examples of your observations
7. Identify ways for the recipient to achieve the new objective or result

EXERCISE

Choose a situation in which you want to give someone feedback. Identify:

What the best time of day/location is to give the feedback

What is already working well

What the desired outcome of the conversation is

What the desired change or new outcome is that you are seeking from the recipient

SUMMARY

- The ability to give masterful feedback is a foundational leadership skill. Done well, it builds trust and connection. When it is given without care, it can create defensiveness and cause the recipient to shut down.
- Following the CARA process and using the appreciative inquiry approach will yield excellent results when the feedback is given with positive intent, kindness and specific examples.
- When giving feedback, be specific by describing observed behaviors and avoid passing on third party observations or comments. Comment only on what you saw, without exaggerating.
- Feedback should be delivered in the moment or soon after.
- Feedback should be given in a loving and compassionate manner with positive intentions for the recipient.

Chapter 9 - Uncovering Your Employees' Values, Beliefs and Motivations

Before I became clear on my values, there were many times in my life when I made decisions based on things that were not truly important to me. There were also times when I knew that I was unhappy, but I was reluctant to admit to myself that I had prioritized the wrong things in my life. Now, whenever I am preparing to make an important decision, I review my beliefs and values to ensure that the decision is in alignment with what is important to me and my future. When decisions are made that don't support my values, it's not long before feelings of boredom, sadness or disappointment arise.

Meaningful Motivation

As a coach leader, you motivate your employees by understanding the values and beliefs that drive them and help co-create opportunities and rewards that are meaningful to them. You do this by paying attention to the language used by your employees to describe their belief systems and what is important them.

You then tailor acknowledgment, rewards and assignments to individual needs.

> The one size fits all reward system fits no one perfectly. As a coach leader, you must treat everyone as an individual — listening for the deep motivation within.

CASE STUDY

Mark was quite stressed about the upcoming relocation of his family. He only had one week to find and purchase a house in a different city. To help make his decision easier, he completed the values exercise to help him decide on the criteria to describe the perfect home for his family. He created a priority list of "essential" and "nice to haves" to help him quickly narrow down his choices.

Among his top five values, was a maximum house price — beyond which he felt that his family would be too stretched financially.

He bought the new house, but did not honor his financial maximum — in fact he exceeded his maximum price by more than 25%. As a result, he has been preoccupied with the cost of the house ever since and wishes that he had stuck to his original criteria.

VALUES

Values are what is important to you. They define who you are and influence all of the choices that you make. They are built through life experiences with family, friends, classmates, teachers, co-workers and sometimes complete strangers. Although your values may change over time, the most lasting and influential values are the ones that you choose freely — not the ones imposed on you or those that you accepted in order to belong to a certain group or organization.

Values are not about statements like, "I should...". Instead, they are about an inner knowledge that something is important or *right* for you. Becoming clear on your values allows you to consciously make choices or changes in your life that reflect who you are. The result is usually less stress and more contentment.

When organizations are clear on their values, they declare them openly and base plans and strategies on them.

MAKING CHOICES

Your values for life, work and relationships should all support each other. Being clear on your values helps you make conscious decisions about issues that affect you.

When you feel stressed, unhappy or are experiencing some other negative emotion, you have three options available to you if you wish to improve your situation. You can:

1. **Leave the Situation**
   - Leave a job or a relationship
   - Disengage from a difficult conversation
2. **Change the situation**
   - Change how you perceive the situation

- Physically change the situation
- Change the dynamics
3. **Fully accept the situation as it is**
   - Unconditional acceptance, without remorse, anger or any other negative emotions

There are no other options if you wish to release the energy-draining thoughts that accompany a conflict. The challenge is to determine which avenue to pursue. This is where a coach can be of great value in helping you to identify options and determine the best way to move forward.

IDENTIFY AND RANK VALUES

People naturally share their values as they speak. Your job as a coach leader is to listen carefully for key words, phrases and energy which indicate that something is important. In addition, you can ask clarifying questions to help your coachee determine if the items are "nice to haves" or "must haves."

Don't waste your time on the unimportant things. Focus on making the few changes that will create the biggest impact.

There are numerous questions that you can ask to help identify and rank values. These include:

- What is important?
- What is most important?
- Is that important for you?
- If you had to choose, what is more important...A or B?
- Is there anything else that you need?
- Is there anything that would make you want to leave that situation? (The coachee must have the "opposite" in place to counter it)
- Do you have any values about that?

REFLECTION

What other questions can you ask to elicit values?

❝❝ A COACHING CONVERSATION (ELICIT VALUES)

Coach: What would you like to focus on today?

Coachee: My son. He is not doing well at school. I don't know what to do about it. I think he is failing all of his courses.

Coach: What would you like to get out of our conversation today?

Coachee: I want to stop fighting with him. I want him to be self-motivated.

Coach: I heard you say that he is not doing well in school, you want to stop fighting with him and you want him to be self-motivated. Which of those do you want to focus on?

Coachee: I don't know. They are all important.

Coach: What is most important right now?

Coachee: I want to stop fighting with him.

Coach: What is the opposite of fighting with him?

Coachee: Having peaceful conversations with him. Not nagging him about school.

Coach: What is the opposite of nagging him?

Coachee: Trusting him and supporting him.

Coach: Do you want to focus on peaceful conversations and trusting and supporting him?

Coachee: Yes. I want to focus on that. I want to improve my relationship with him.

.... ❞❞

EXERCISE: LISTEN FOR VALUES

Listen for values during your discussions over the next few days and try to determine what is "essential" and what is "nice to have."

What words or phrases did you hear that described your coachee's values?

What did you notice in your coachee when you helped her to enunciate and clarify her values?

"Don't believe everything you hear – even in your own mind."
Daniel G. Amen, M.D.

TESTIMONIAL

"Prior to my first coach training, I was easily influenced by others in my decisions and in my definition of right or wrong. After I completed my training, I was clearer about what I wanted in my life. Once I gained clarity, I did not care what others thought. Now I know what is important and what is not. I discovered that what is important to me in my personal evolution are: relationships, integrity and doing what brings me joy and ease. I know that I can stand independently, and I want to increasingly do this with grace."
Sandy

BELIEFS

Have you ever considered the impact of your beliefs on the way you live your life? Most times, beliefs are useful and can help you to achieve amazing things. For example, the simple act of believing that you are good at math can help you to be more tenacious in finding a solution. Conversely, if you believe that you are not good at math, you may give up too soon.

What would life be like if some of your beliefs were not true?

What if only believing in them makes them true?

On a daily basis, you may be limiting your life to match your beliefs; this in turn reinforces the beliefs that you hold.

ELICITING BELIEFS USING COACHING QUESTIONS

An important part of your job as a coach is to help your coachees understand the impact of their beliefs on their lives.

Listen carefully for key phrases that define other people's beliefs. These include:

- "I am not good at...."
- "I could never do...."
- "I will always be...."
- "My mother was _____ and I inherited it"
- "I feel an obligation to...."
- "I am really strong"
- "I am a good reader"

All of those phrases offer excellent opportunities to explore beliefs.

Sometimes people confuse beliefs with facts. For example, the following likely are 100% true.

- "I am _____ years old."
- "I am male/female."
- "I have two vertebrae fused together."
- "I am _____ tall."

Unfortunately, we can develop beliefs that are not 100% true and assume that they are facts. For example:

- "Since I am now _____ years old, it is no longer appropriate for me to...."
- "As a woman, I should be ...."
- "I can't do _____ because of my back"
- "I am too short for..."

Even though the coachee's beliefs may be widely accepted in society or her social structure, they may not be true. These are called limiting beliefs. Dr. Wayne Dyer calls them excuses. By reassessing limiting beliefs, the coachee may find more opportunities than she previously believed existed.

If your coachee states:

Coachee: I will never have enough money for a down payment on a house.

If she truly believes that it is impossible to save for a down payment, then she won't be looking for possibilities to build it. Probe to determine if the belief is true:

Coach: What would be possible if that was not 100% true?
Coachee: It may take longer than I hoped, but I believe that there are ways to save up enough money for a down payment on a house.

When she sees the world through this new lens, she will be more open to possibilities such as:

- Foregoing the daily $5 coffee and pastry
- Setting a monthly/yearly limit on clothing purchases
- Following a food budget
- Taking a second job
- Applying for a promotion or new job

There are usually many possibilities when you are open to them. If, on the other hand, you believe that your goal is not possible, then the ideas generated may feel like pointless restrictions rather than opportunities.

If your coachee identifies a limiting belief, you can ask:

- Is that really true?
- Whose belief is that?
- Is that 100% true?
- Where did that belief come from?
- Is that a belief that serves you well?
- Do you want to keep that belief?
- Really?

Once the coachee understands that her beliefs may not be 100% true, her next step is to create new beliefs that expand her possibilities.

- If that was not true, what would be possible?
- What is the opposite of that?
- If you could do that, how would that change things?
- It may not be easy, but what if you *could* achieve that?

Beliefs should be challenged when they prevent the coachee from moving towards her desired outcome.

REFLECTION

What additional questions can you use to elicit or clarify beliefs?

*"You are what
you believe
yourself to be."*
Paulo Coelho

EXERCISE

In your next coaching conversation, probe to ensure that possibilities for action and next steps are aligned with your coachee's beliefs and values.

REFLECTION

Were you able to link your coachee's action steps to her beliefs and values?

What did you notice in your coachee when you helped her to enunciate and clarify her beliefs and values?

What words or phrases did you hear that described your coachee's beliefs and values?

66 A COACHING CONVERSATION (ELICITING BELIEFS)

....

Coach: What are your beliefs about your relationship with your son?

Coachee: (long pause) Great question. I don't think I can be a parent and his teacher at the same time. I want to focus on the longer term relationship. He is making his own choices. Eventually school will be done and I want to still have a relationship with him.

Coach: Do you need to be both his parent and his teacher?

Coachee: Hmmm, I definitely want to be his parent. I think that maybe the school is up to him at this point. I can create good conditions for working, maybe even find some way to motivate him, but really, the motivation has to come from him.

Coach: What are your beliefs about motivation?

Coachee: I think that if a person is self-motivated, then that is much better than punishments and threats.

Coach: What does that tell you?

Coachee: I have been nagging him instead of building a strong relationship with him. I actually don't even know what would motivate him to try harder.

Coach: How could you know?

Coachee: I can ask him...

Coach: How would you do that?

Coachee: (long pause) I would say something like, 'Pat, we have been fighting a lot and I want to change that. I am your mother, not your teacher and I want to have a long term relationship with you. What is it that you need from me to improve in school?'

Coach: How does that feel?

Coachee: Scary. It feels like I am giving up control.

Coach: Control?

Coachee: Yikes - what a nightmare for my son if I am trying to control him.

Coach: What would be even better?

Coachee: Like I said earlier, trust, peace, self-motivation.

Coach: What is holding you back from that?

Coachee: I guess a belief that I am responsible for his outcome.

Coach: Are you?

Coachee: No. All that I can do is provide the best conditions for studying and try and find out what would motivate him.

Coach: So...

Coachee: I need to say that to him.

Coach: How would that be?

Coachee: So much less pressure — on both of us.

....

LINKING RESOURCES AND ACTION STEPS TO BELIEFS AND VALUES

When you discuss resources and actions, it is important for the chosen outcomes to be aligned with the coachee's core beliefs and values.

Values Questions

- What is important about that resource?
- How does that align with your values?
- On a scale of 1 to 10, how motivated are you to achieve that?
- How important is it to do that?
- How does that action fit in with your core values?

Beliefs Questions

- Is that really true?
- How do you know that to be true?
- What if that wasn't true?
- What if there were no limits?
- Does that fit into your belief system?

MOTIVATION

Once you know what is important for your coachee, do your best to provide her with what she wants. If your coachee wants to improve her writing skills, provide her opportunities to write. If she has kids in daycare who need to be picked up at a certain time, don't schedule meetings that interfere with that.

If you are finding it difficult to discern a coachee's values and beliefs, ask.

- What is important to you?
- What do you value?
- Where do you want to be in 5 years? What skills will get you there?
- What do you think you need to work on?
- What assignments are you most interested in?
- How can I best support you?
- What do you need?
- What kind of feedback are you looking for?

For long-term growth, translate this information into a yearly training and development plan that is reviewed on a regular basis.

66 A COACHING CONVERSATION

Notice the beliefs, values and motivations.

Coach: What would you like to focus on today?

Coachee: I hate my job. I don't have any passion for it anymore. I am working 80-hour work weeks and barely making enough money to survive. I want to sell my business, but I don't want everyone in town to know because they will stop buying memberships. I just want out as soon as possible.

Coach: What is the most important thing to focus on today?

Coachee: I want to talk about how to structure the sale. Do I sell the whole building, do I rent out the space, do I hire a manager...there are so many possibilities, and I feel overwhelmed. I might make a horrible decision because I want out so bad.

Coach: What will tell you at the end of our conversation that you have what you need?

Coachee: I will be clear on the best way for me to move on that includes my long term needs.

Coach: What will that 'look like' or what will you have?

Coachee: A clear idea of the structure and who I will target to find the buyer or new manager.

Coach: What are your first thoughts?

Coachee: I could sell the whole building, I could lease out just the space that I use for my business or I could hire a manager to manage my business. The equipment that I have purchased is very expensive. It would be hard for someone to come up with that amount of money right away. I could do a gradual increase in rent to get them started.

Coach: You have put a lot of thought into this already. What is most important?

Coachee: I really need to move on as soon as possible, but I want the business to be successful. I built this business over the past 25 years, and I will continue to live in this town. I don't want to let people down.

Coach: What defines a successful business?

Coachee: There will be a buzz around the place, the new owner will have

"Courage doesn't always roar. Sometimes courage is the little voice at the end of the day that says I'll try again tomorrow."
Mary Anne Radmacher

energy and attract people. There will be enough money to pay the rent and live comfortably. There will be new revenue streams. The space will be updated and attractive. I just don't care about that stuff anymore.

Coach: What kind of structure would best lead towards that successful outcome?

Coachee: The person needs to have enough money invested so that they don't bail out if they don't make money right away. The person probably needs to be younger than me. The person should have some business experience and know how to use new software and social media. I just don't have the interest in that and nowadays you need that.

Coach: What does that tell you?

Coachee: Just leasing out the space is not enough incentive to keep the person if things are not going well right away. I think that the person needs to buy the business from me as well as lease the space. I have 25 years of experience building up clientele, gathering email addresses and contact information, the place is already set up for the new person. They have to pay to take it over. I want it to be enough so they don't walk away too easily, but at the same time, not so much that it is unaffordable. My main interest is in moving on. As long as they pay enough in rent for the space and the equipment, I will be happy.

Coach: What is the belief that you hold about that?

Coachee: Just like buying a house, there is a reason banks ask for a down payment. It is so you don't walk away when the going gets tough.

Coach: What is important about the owner not walking away?

Coachee: My reputation and responsibility to my clients. Also, if the business fails, then I won't get to collect rent. I want someone who will be committed to making the business work, not just dabbling in this.

Coach: How much is enough?

Coachee: I have no idea.

Coach: How could you find out?

Coachee: I can talk to my accountant for a suggestion and talk to the owner of a similar business who did the same thing.

Coach: Before narrowing down to the final option, do you want to explore the other possibilities?

Coachee: My first thoughts are that I don't want to sell the building. It is my retirement money. It is just not an option. I also don't want to hire a manager. I want to completely separate myself. The only option is leasing the space and charging a buy-in fee.

Coach: Are you sure that there are not other options?

Coachee: I can't think of any.

Coach: (pause)

Coachee: Okay, there is one more option. Hiring a manager and part of his or her compensation is based on total sales.

Coach: How does that one sound?

Coachee: Not good. I want out.

Coach: Are there any other options?

Coachee: I could break the space into smaller pieces.

Coach: How does that sound?

Coachee: I don't even want to go there. I have equipment that fits in this space. I want the equipment rental to be part of the deal. It cost me a lot of money to buy.

Coach: Anything else?

Coachee: No. I want to focus on getting a buy-in price to sell the business and rent the space.

Coach: Are you sure?

Coachee: Yes.

Coach: What are your next steps?

Coachee: I will talk to my accountant about suggestions for the buy-in price and talk to my colleague who sold his business.

Coach: Is there anything you want to do?

Coachee: I need to start preparing the package that describes the offer.

Coach: Anything else?

Coachee: I will start calling around to see if there are people who may interested.

Coach: Are there any other actions?

Coachee: No.

Coach: What is your time line to get these things done?

Coachee: I will talk to my accountant at our meeting tomorrow. I will ask his help to complete the package by the end of the month. I will call my colleague later today.

Coach: What would you like to tell me when we meet next week?

Coachee: That I have a price established for the buy-in and a monthly lease rate. We have an outline for the package and have started work on it. We have the financial information in it, a description of the property and the equipment and the potential income. I will have talked to my colleague. I will scout out potential buyers.

Coach: How does this fit in with your long term goals?

Coachee: Perfectly. I have new interests. I want to move on.

Coach: You wanted to outline a clear structure and potential buyer. How are you feeling about your accomplishments today?

Coachee: I can't find the buyer until I define what I am selling and for how much. I can generate some interest, but until the package is prepared, I can't really look for a serious buyer.

Coach: How are you feeling now about the business?

Coachee: Really good. I was feeling overwhelmed when we started, but I can see where this is going.

Coach: What are you taking away from our conversation?

Coachee: I want a buyer who can't easily walk away. I want it to be a fair deal so he or she can be successful, but they need that down payment to keep them from walking away too easily. "

SUMMARY

- Beliefs and values are developed based on the family you were born into, key people in your life and significant life events.
- Beliefs and values drive our behaviors, decisions and emotions.
- Beliefs and values can change over time based on significant life events (or through coaching).
- Coachees disclose their beliefs and values through their language and actions.
- Uncovering your coachee's beliefs and values is a key element of coaching.
- In order to create transformation, supporting actions need to be in alignment with core beliefs and values.
- Creating new beliefs can be key to expanding the coachee's range of possibilities.

Chapter 10 - Acknowledgment

People who are masterful at acknowledgment listen carefully to what is important to others, then look for ways to acknowledge them when the other person has done things or made choices that support those values or goals. For example, if I knew that one of my coachees was working towards improving her ability to connect with others, then I would find ways to acknowledge that behavior. If, instead, I focused on acknowledging her ability to plan meetings, I might miss the mark and acknowledge something that has little value for her.

Acknowledgment is a cornerstone for my colleague, John. When speaking with others, he pays careful attention to what is important to that person, then looks for ways to provide acknowledgment that is tailored to the person's particular needs. He does not assume that people want to be compensated in the same way (e.g. money) — instead, he asks questions like:

- What would make this worthwhile for you?
- How do you want to be acknowledged?

- What is important for you?

His strategy works. People who work with him usually end up working with him for 25 years or more. They are very loyal and feel appreciated for the work that they do.

ACKNOWLEDGMENT

Acknowledgment is the act of recognizing who a person is, what is important to that person and affirming achievements that are important to her. Praise is a way of offering approval and judgment. An example of praise is: "You did a really good job." An example of acknowledgment is: "I want to acknowledge the courage it took for you to stand up for yourself when your colleague tried to pass off your ideas as her own. I know that standing up for yourself has been a challenge for you in the past."

When you acknowledge someone you:

- Use a specific example
- Don't use superlatives (e.g. "great," or "fantastic")
- Acknowledge a behavior or action that is meaningful to the recipient

> Acknowledgment can be used to build a strong resource anchor in the coachee when the coach reminds or enlightens her about her strengths and past accomplishments.

The coach does not *praise* the coachee, but rather helps her to recall her own actions, the courage it took to enable those actions and the final results.

To feel acknowledged, the coachee must first believe she is

worthy of acknowledgment. If that is not present, the coachee will not hear or integrate the acknowledgment. For some people, this means that they need to build up a positive feeling over an extended period of time with numerous cumulative acts of being acknowledged (by self and others).

After acknowledging your coachee ask:

- How does that land for you?
- How does that feel?
- What did you hear?

> To be meaningful, the coach should acknowledge the coachee in areas in which the *coachee* wants to be acknowledged. Conversely, if the coach acknowledges the coachee for something that is not meaningful for her, it can break rapport.

Using the principles of AI and masterful feedback will naturally set you up to create a cycle of meaningful acknowledgment. When practicing acknowledgment be sure to be:

- Sincere
- Specific
- Honest
- Kind
- Compassionate

Some of your coachees may not be accustomed to receiving acknowledgment. Notice their reactions and speak in language that is meaningful to them. Avoid using superfluous language (e.g. "great" or "excellent") because that infers that the person providing acknowledgment is judging the other person. It does not help the recipient understand the behavior that was valued nor how it contributed to the organization or event.

How to Acknowledge Your Coachee

There are many ways to acknowledge your coachees. These include:

1. Acknowledge Strengths

When you acknowledge strengths, you highlight your coachee's abilities and accomplishments. You do this by asking or reminding the coachee what she is doing well. By building upon those strengths, your coachee develops more confidence and a positive outlook. This opens the door to even more courage and willingness to grow.

Focusing on strengths does not mean ignoring weak areas. Rather, you manage the weak areas, but don't focus entirely on them. When extracting lessons from weaknesses, rebuild confidence by helping your client remember or identify her strengths, then link those strengths to the desired outcome.

 ....

Coach: What worked well for you over the past week?
Coachee: I finished writing my plan. I am really proud of myself. It wasn't easy, but I just set aside the time and got to work.
Coach: Congratulations. I know that it was really important for you to finish it this week so you can focus on the end year reports. I also know that it is not your favorite activity.
....

2. Facilitate the Ability to Be Open to New Possibilities

By acknowledging a coachee's past successes and accomplishments, the coach can facilitate the ability in the coachee to be open to possibilities. For example, if a coachee arrives at the coaching meeting in an unresourceful state, she may not be able to appreciate the range of possibilities open to her. When the coach takes the time to acknowledge the coachee's strengths and past successes, the coachee will be in a more resourceful frame of mind to envision and enunciate bolder outcomes.

 ....

Coachee: I am so discouraged. I just can't seem to get anything right lately. I missed the deadline for the delivery. I don't see a way out of this mess.
*Coach: I can see that you are pretty discouraged and feeling like there is no way out right now. Can we take a moment to acknowledge some things that **are** going well?*
Coachee: Yes.
Coach: Can you tell me what worked well for you over the past week?
Coachee: I did a good job of preparing for —— and facilitating —— two meetings. My boss commented specifically on that.
Coach: What else went well this week?
Coachee: (slight change in body language) My boss told me that the report I prepared was very useful — especially the supporting graphs and data.
....

3. Mirror and Reflect

When the coach repeats or paraphrases the coachee's words, the coachee can provide corrections or acknowledge their validity. This provides greater clarity, which can, in turn, be a catalyst for new ideas and outcomes.

 ....

Coach: How does it feel to acknowledge yourself?
Coachee: It feels weird.
Coach: Weird?
Coachee: Yes. Awkward.
Coach: Can you accept that you did a good job of preparing for and facilitating the meetings, and that the report you submitted was useful?
Coachee: Yes. I did a good job of facilitating. The report really was good. (smile)
Coach: Let that sink in for a moment.
....

4. Acknowledge How the Coachee's Words and Actions Affect You

If during the coaching meeting the coach feels that there is resistance to a question, the coach may choose to acknowledge this feeling and comment on it to the coachee. The outcome could be validation of the feeling (if the coach's intuition was correct) or increased self-awareness for the coachee (if she responds that it wasn't resistance, but rather some other emotion).

 ....

(Coachee is having trouble acknowledging herself)

Coach: How are you feeling now?

Coachee: Kind of uncomfortable. I am not used to doing this.

Coach: I can see that you are uncomfortable. Would you be willing to give it a try?

Coachee: Yes.

Coach: Go ahead and picture yourself being appreciated by the team members and your boss for facilitating the meetings, being organized and handing in a useful report...breathe it in...how does that feel?

Coachee: Pretty good. I did a good job.

....

5. Hold the Coachee Accountable to the Vision/Goals

As coach, you are responsible for keeping the client on track by moving her towards her vision/goals. Masterful coaches co-create a cycle of success by continuously assisting the coachee to link accomplishments to the desired goals, while revising and reinforcing the future vision with each new lesson.

- How does this fit with your vision/goal?
- What is important here?
- How can you link that learning to your vision/goal?

"" ....

Coach: How does that fit with your goal of being more comfortable as a leader in your new role?

Coachee: Baby steps. If I can do more of those small things, I will feel even more comfortable.

Coach: What other small things would bring you closer to your goal?

Coachee: Doing those small things with more confidence, which is already building. I am not there yet, but I can see where this is going.

Coach: Can you create a picture of where you want to be?

Coachee: Yes. Even more confidence. I am not surprised when people are happy with my performance. I know I am good at what I do.

""

....

6. Believe in Your Coachee's Abilities and Potential

If you truly believe that your coachee is capable of or has the potential to achieve her vision and goals, you will behave in a manner that catalyzes her inner power. You can keep her moving forward with questions like:

*   What do you need to make this happen?
*   What is holding you back from ....?

"" ....

Coach: What else would help you achieve your goal?

Coachee: Being more accepting of myself when I make mistakes.

Coach: How can you do that?

Coachee: Like you said before, failure is only feedback. It is how we learn.

Coach: Do you believe that?

Coachee: I believe it for others, but have a hard time accepting it for me.

Coach: How would you grow if you did not make mistakes?

Coachee: (pause) Good question. I would be playing it too safe. I guess I need to work on how to make those decisions. When to take risks.

Coach: How would you know that?

""

....

7. Encourage the Coachee to Celebrate Her Successes

Don't wait until the end of the process to celebrate your coachee's successes. Instead, encourage her to celebrate the milestones that will lead towards the desired outcome. Potential questions include:

- What would be a meaningful way for you to celebrate that milestone?
- How can you acknowledge that success?
- Take a moment to acknowledge that outcome.

 ....

Coach: How can you acknowledge that success?

Coachee: I need to accept that I can do good work and people appreciate it.

Coach: How does that feel?

Coachee: Pretty good. I don't need to keep proving myself. I am already good at what I do.

Coach: How do you know that?

Coachee: Partly by how I compare my work with others, but mostly that I get feedback that my work is good.

Coach: What specifically is good?

Coachee: Clear, concise reports. I am easy to get along with. I am not afraid to admit when I don't know something.

Coach: How does that land for you?

Coachee: Weird but good. I need to just relax and enjoy this job instead of nitpicking myself.

Coach: Relax and enjoy your job. How good would that be?

Coachee: That would be perfect.

....

SUMMARY

- Acknowledgment is the act of recognizing who a person is, what is important to her and affirming achievements that are important to her.
- Acknowledgment can be used to build a strong resource anchor in the coachee when the coach reminds or enlightens her about her strengths and past accomplishments.
- To be meaningful, the coach should acknowledge the coachee in areas in which *the coachee* wants to be acknowledged.

Chapter 11 - Become a Coach Leader

"One day you will wake up and there won't be any more time to do the things you've always wanted. Do it now."
Paulo Coelho

When I look back to my early twenties, I realize now how much I would have benefitted from both undergoing coach training and engaging a coach to work with me. At the time, I was one of a few women in the Canadian Armed Forces serving as a combat arms officer. Although the vast majority of the people that I worked with were supportive and helpful, there were a small number of people who resisted having a woman in this role. These people challenged me in ways that sometimes created frustration and anger. I did not have a safe person to confide in, so I started getting quite concerned with *not making mistakes*; this, clearly, is not a healthy way to operate. Everyone makes mistakes — it is part of how we learn.

My role models were all men, and I faced challenges that they could not relate to. Having a coach would have helped me to relax more authentically into my role, discuss and resolve the problems that I was facing and let go of worrying about making mistakes. I would not have changed anything about my experiences because they made me who I am today, but I could have moved through the challenges more quickly and enjoyed my job a lot more than I did.

"Just prior to departing for a three week holiday, my controller resigned unexpectedly. In the past this would have derailed my vacation plans. Instead of focusing on the problem, I focused on what I needed and engaged my controller to help me find the solution. Together we identified the next steps.

We worked together to update the company values, vision and job description. My current controller was then delegated the authority to advertise and interview for her replacement in my absence. I left for my vacation feeling relaxed and confident that the hiring process was in good hands.

Upon return, I interviewed then hired the top candidate recommended by my former controller. I don't think I could have found a better candidate myself."

John

"Wearing a mask wears you out. Faking it is fatiguing. The most exhausting activity is pretending to be what you know you aren't."
Rick Warren

BECOME A COACH LEADER

The coach approach is rapidly becoming an expected approach to leadership. The question is not *if* you should become a coach leader, but *how* to become one. While coaching is not right for all situations, there are many benefits for you, your employees and your organization when this approach is learned and used appropriately.

BENEFITS TO THE COACH LEADER

Delegate More – With Better Results

When you use the coach approach, in conjunction with clear decision-making protocols, you can delegate more work, thereby leaving you free to plan, network, liaise and complete other tasks. Delegation develops future leaders in your organization, which provides the organization with more resiliency and depth in the long term.

Be Yourself

There is nothing more powerful than being yourself. Being someone who you are not takes a lot of energy. Worrying about how you are *supposed* to behave or making mistakes is exhausting. By being yourself, you can relax, pay attention to what you are feeling and draw upon your emotions and intuition to make better decisions. This will allow you to connect with people at a new level.

Less Nagging

By improving your listening skills, you will notice the energy in other people's voices and body language, which will enable you to ask questions that bring more ideas to the surface. When others are invited to participate in decisions, they become part-owner of the ideas and the outcomes. This catalyzes enthusiasm and leads to more engagement.

Less Drama

When you develop the skills to engage in difficult conversations, you will be able to discuss and resolve issues before they get explosive. Gradually, others will follow your lead and initiate their own conversations as problems arise.

More Clarity

As a coach leader, you learn communications excellence. This includes mastering how you deliver and receive messages by asking questions to clarify meaning and promote understanding.

BENEFITS TO THE EMPLOYEES

Employees Will Be Heard

People want to be heard and acknowledged. They want to be a valued part of the organization. By taking the time to listen to other people's ideas, complaints and future goals you will be able to acknowledge your employees and encourage even more of the behaviors that you are looking for. When people feel appreciated, they are more willing to deliver even more.

Employees Will Become Better Decision Makers

By listening to your employees' concerns, asking questions to flush out their ideas, and delegating decision-making power, you will create empowered and enthusiastic employees. Allowing them to make mistakes within predetermined boundaries will help them become better decision-makers.

Employees Will be More Engaged

A problem today is that people are absent while *at* work (e.g. on Facebook, internet, etc.). By engaging your employees in the generation of ideas and decisions, they will have more interest in their outcomes and will be naturally more engaged.

More Honesty and Truthfulness

Coach leaders learn to discuss difficult topics with grace. Problems can then be resolved while they are still small — without hurting people's feelings.

BENEFITS TO THE ORGANIZATION

Less Turnover

Some of the reasons why people leave organizations are:

- They are not engaged
- There is an unpleasant work atmosphere
- They don't see a career path
- They don't feel acknowledged

Coach leaders create an atmosphere in which employees can approach them to deal with these issues before they become insurmountable.

Integrated Goals and Vision

Coach leaders learn how to help their teams and employees integrate their personal goals and growth plans with those of the organization. This ensures that everyone is working towards a common vision — with individual needs being met along the way.

More Productivity

Coach leaders clearly define team member's decision making powers and help resolve petty arguments before they derail the group. The coach leader acknowledges both the team and the individuals for their efforts on a regular basis.

A Coaching Culture is Developed

An organization will benefit tremendously as employees naturally improve their own communications and leadership skills by emulating the behaviors of the coach leader. Employees' decision-making skills will improve and their confidence will soar as they take on more responsibility and receive acknowledgment for their successes.

" A COACHING CONVERSATION

Coach: How would you like to use our time together today?

Coachee: I have learned some amazing new coaching skills, but I am just not sure how to start using them at my job. I have a successful career already, and I am reluctant to start messing with things now when things are going well.

Coach: What is working well for you now?

Coachee: I am really organized, I put a lot of time and effort into keeping things well planned, I am on top of everyone's tasks and we are always ahead of schedule.

Coach: That sounds pretty good. How do you feel about your work? (This question takes the coachee out of her head and into her body.)

Coachee: Well, I guess that is the problem. Although I am doing well and get excellent performance reviews, I don't think I can keep up this pace for much longer. I am exhausted by the time I get home, and I am too tired to exercise and spend time with my family. I think about work in the middle of the night.

Coach: If you could have it all, how would the picture look instead?

Coachee: I would have lots of energy for work, be organized, but pace myself so that I also have lots of energy for home. I also want to get home earlier. Maybe even carve out some time for exercising. To be honest, that all seems ambitious. I just don't know how I can achieve that.

Coach: I heard, 'energy for work, energy for home, manageable pace and time for exercise'. If I said the word balance, would that resonate for you?

Coachee: Balance. (Laughs) It seems impossible right now, but yes, that is what I want. I don't want to live this way anymore.

Coach: What would you like to have at the end of the conversation that will help you to create a balanced life?

Coachee: Good question. (Pause) Since my work life seems to be dictating the energy levels in the rest of my life, I think that I need to look at how to make that part of my life easier. I still want to do my job well, but maybe I can do it with less effort.

Coach: What would you have that you don't have now that will enable that?

Coachee: I guess I need to re-think the whole work thing. My approach. I do know that change is possible. I have learned about the coach approach, but I just don't know how to make it work for me.

Coach: Am I hearing that you want to learn how to integrate the coach approach to help create balance and reduce your energy output at work?

Coachee: Yes.

Coach: At the end of our conversation, what do you want to have that will set that in motion?

Coachee: I would like to have a picture of what it would be like to integrate the new coaching skills and have a few first steps towards achieving that.

Coach: What will your life be like in 20 years if you carry on the way you are now?

Coachee: It is depressing to imagine another 20 years of this.

Coach: If you could have it all, what would be different in 20 years?

Coachee: More peace, more fun, more balance. I will have good health and a good family life, too.

Coach: From what you know about the coach approach, what can you imagine that would support your needs?

Coachee: I have a picture of work being quite a bit different than it is now. I am picturing a lot more peace. I can see myself looking a lot more relaxed, having a lot more fun and spending more time talking with people, supporting them and developing them instead of doing it all myself.

Coach: (pause)

Coachee: (big breath) I am seeing everyone happier, not just me. I am seeing that I could be a really great leader that people want to work with because I don't micromanage, but I also don't just let people flounder. Somehow I have a balance of keeping in touch, but letting them do their own thing. There is trust and a knowing of the other person's skills and abilities.

Coach: How is that?

Coachee: That looks so much better than what I am doing now. I would enjoy my job so much more, and I would be developing new leaders. It all just seems so much more satisfying

Coach: When you see that picture, what do you notice about the things that you are doing to make it happen?

Coachee: I see that I am comfortable enough to be myself. I don't pretend that I know things or feel like I need to show people how amazing I am. I can share the spot light with others. I am just calm, I talk to people and I notice more than I do now. I notice people's moods, their excitement, their sadness and I can connect to that. That is what is different - I connect with people and find ways to motivate them deep inside instead of boss them around like I do now.

Coach: What else do you see yourself doing to make it happen?

Coachee: Well, I just see myself more relaxed. When I notice things, I ask about them. It is not a confrontation; I simply ask from a place of caring about them.

Coach: Hmmm - how is that?

Coachee: Not as hard as I was thinking. I was making things harder than it needed to be. Trying to remember the CARA process, the appreciative inquiry process, about somatic coaching, etc. etc.

Coach: What if it was easy and a lot less effort, what principles would drive that for you?

Coachee: Really it is more of a mind-set than techniques. Even if I can't remember the CARA steps - and really, how hard is that? All I need to think about is being, watching others, being curious and being caring. If I can listen, ask what is important and help others be successful, then everything else will work out. The conversations will be easier, even if I don't know the 'techniques'. That is not what is important.

Coach: If you could summarize the most important things, what would they be?

Coachee: Being present. Being me. Being curious. Caring and developing others.

Coach: How will you do that....easily?

Coachee: I will start seeing my employees with a different lens. I am there to support them. If I am caring, it will allow me to have the deep conversations.

Coach: Is there anything specific you need to make that happen?

Coachee: Maybe over the next week, I will focus on just one or two things that will make the biggest difference. (Pause) I think that the most important things to focus on are connecting with people and finding out what is important to them through genuine conversations. I think that will be a good start.

Coach: How will you do that?

Coachee: Each day I will go and talk with each of my employees. No pressure. Just connect, see how they are doing and what is going on in their lives. I can't push them, I need to create a connection at their pace. I will listen for what they are focusing on and notice their energy to see how important it is for them.

Coach: Can you picture that?

Coachee: Yes, I can.

Coach: How are you feeling about integrating the coaching skills while maintaining or improving your success?

Coachee: So much better. I can't do it all at once, but I can start doing small things. It is more about the way I think, not about following an exact process.

Coach: What would you like to tell me when we meet next week?

Coachee: That each day I made a small connection with each employee. That I am starting to understand what is important for each of them. They are starting to see me differently.

Coach: What are you taking away from today's conversation?

Coachee: It can be overwhelming if I try to do it all at once. I can just do one small step at a time and slowly make my way to becoming the kind of leader I want to be. 🙶

"As coaching continues its evolution in organizations, there appears to be a trend from leaders being coached to leaders being coaches."
MetrixGlobal

PUTTING IT ALL TOGETHER

Becoming a coach leader begins with your mind-set. Coaches have the ability to see possibilities in their coachees that the coachees themselves cannot even imagine. By approaching the relationship from a place of caring you find out what is important for your coachee, then acknowledge and reinforce it.

As a coach leader, you are comfortable not knowing the answer. You set parameters, then let go of your attachment to the outcome. Be prepared to be pleasantly surprised at what your coachees dream up.

When you understand the potential of appreciative inquiry, you naturally encourage your coachees to focus on what they *want*, rather than on the problem. This completely changes the mood of the conversation.

You soon start to realize that intention is more important than technique. Simply paying attention to feelings, emotions and intuition allows you connect with people at a different level.

Being curious, yet respectful, allows you to get to know other people's hopes and dreams. By supporting them in the achievement of these goals, you empower them and catalyze an energy and enthusiasm that helps them become who they want to be.

Don't overthink it. Just do it. Just *be* a coach leader. The rest will follow.

HOW TO BECOME A COACH LEADER

Read this Book

If you read this book, do the exercises and take time to reflect, you will understand the coach mindset, have a simple protocol and have many ideas on how to integrate the coach approach to leadership.

There are many coaching books available to suit your needs and preferences. Read as many as you can, and integrate the ideas and techniques that fit with your beliefs, values and leadership approach.

Start Small

Choose safe situations and practice one element of coaching at a time. Make it transparent that you are learning the coaching protocol, ask permission and seek opportunities to practice.

One safe way to learn is by bartering coaching services with another coach. You not only benefit from receiving coaching, but you can also receive feedback on your coaching from your partner.

Hire a Coach

Engage a coach to help you become a coach leader. This allows you to focus on one new technique or theory at a time and to integrate the coach approach in a way that is authentic to you.

Take a Coach Training Program

Sign up for an introductory coaching program to learn how to coach from experienced coaches. In addition to learning coaching tools and techniques, you will improve your skills by receiving and implementing changes based on feedback from experienced coaches.

Search the Web

Watch coaching demonstrations on You Tube, read coaching web sites, join coaching forums. Read the International Coach Federation website and learn more about the coaching profession.

Be Transparent

Tell people that you plan on introducing the coach approach. Share articles and tell them what you are doing. Be clear about when you are using the coach approach and when you are not.

Be a Coach

Don't just use coaching tools, start looking at your situation with the eyes of a coach. Always think about how you can bring out the best in others through the use of questions and the delegation of decisions.

Keep it Simple

Be curious and start asking questions. Allow yourself to *not know* the answers. This is a powerful place to be as it takes the pressure off of you to know all of the answers and helps to develop other future leaders.

Just Do It

Failure is only feedback. Just give it a try. Tell people that you are practicing introductory coaching skills, and then ***just do it.*** If you pay attention to other people's body language, approach conversations from a place of love and compassion and genuinely want the best for others, you will be successful in integrating the coach approach.

APPENDICES

Appendix 1 - The CARA Process

The CARA process employs four steps:

- **Connection**: This stage involves creating a safe environment, rapport and a meaningful connection with the coachee. It is important to take the time needed to connect with your coachee—if she does not trust, she may not be able to move towards resolving her issue at anything deeper than a superficial level.
- **Awareness**: This stage involves helping the coachee to experience her topic clearly and objectively. It is important to take the time to ensure that the coachee is working on the most important topic at hand, or you will achieve only mediocre or superficial results.
- **Resources**: This stage involves helping the coachee to investigate new possibilities of action and to increase her resourcefulness.
- **Action**: This stage involves turning the results of the resource stage into action steps with clear and measurable outcomes. It also includes a summary of the key learning points (takeaways).

The CARA process is not linear. You can move freely between the steps to meet your coachee's needs in the best way possible.

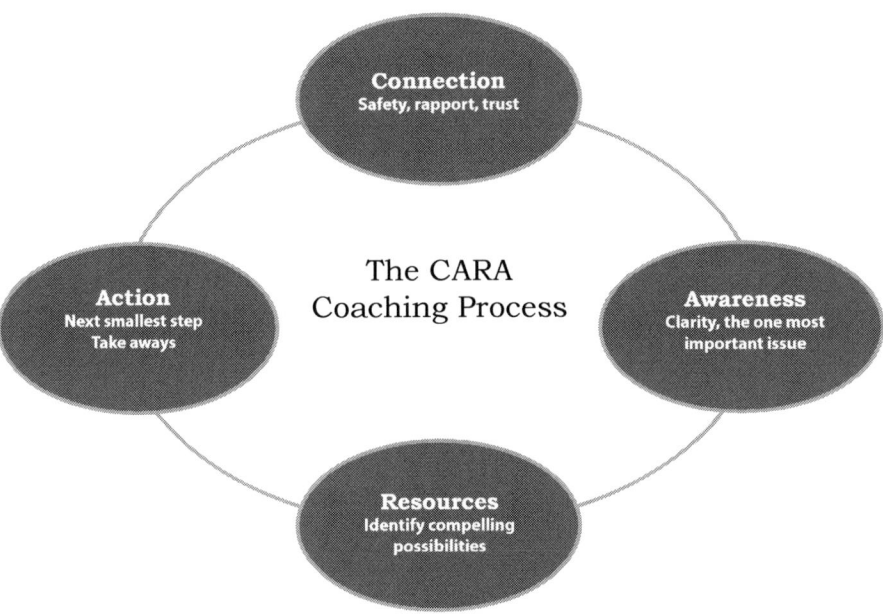

The CARA
Coaching Process

Connection
Safety, rapport, trust

Awareness
Clarity, the one most
important issue

Resources
Identify compelling
possibilities

Action
Next smallest step
Take aways

Appendix 2 - Centering Exercises

Exercise: Simple Breathing

- Sit upright in your chair or stand
- Place your feet hip-width apart
- Place your hands in your lap or let them hang freely
- Relax your shoulders
- Close your eyes
- Notice your breath going in and out
- Pay attention to your breath for a few minutes
- When your mind wanders, simply bring your attention back to your breath

Exercise: Abdominal Breathing

- Sit up tall with one hand on your navel, the other on your knee
- Relax your belly
- Close your eyes
- Inhale deeply through your nose so that the hand over your navel is pushed outward (your belly should swell like a balloon)
- Exhale deeply through your nose and notice how your navel comes back in towards your spine
- Relax your belly even more
- Breathe deeply without forcing the breath
- Continue for a couple of minutes

APPENDIX 3 - THE ACCOUNTABILITY SEQUENCE

1. Negotiate the Meeting Agreement

The coach guides the coachee to achieving closure on her meeting agreement.

- **Topic**: What the coachee wants to focus on
- **Outcome**: What the coachee want to get out of the conversation

2. Action Steps and Accountability

After exploring the topic and possibilities, the coachee clearly identifies her next steps (actions). These steps should be concisely summarized, measurable, time-bound and relevant to moving forward on the meeting agreement.

3. Accountability to the Agreement

Sometimes options and possibilities sound good until it is time to implement them. The discussion of accountability is intended to create a way to keep the coachee "answerable" to her commitment. It also ensures that the coachee has sufficient internal motivation to complete the next steps. The coach's role is to test the coachee's readiness and help her overcome obstacles to success. It can be helpful to create a future vision of success

4. Wrap-Up

Before closing the meeting, ask the coachee what she has learned that will help her to move forward with her topic. This reinforces the awareness that was generated during the coaching meeting and helps to solidify why her next steps are important to generate forward movement.

5. Follow-Up

At your next meeting, ask your coachee to update you on the actions that she committed to. If, for example, the coachee has not had the conversation that she committed to, a coachable moment is there to be seized. There is value in exploring the explanation from the perspective of uncovering a blind spot in the coachee. Be sure to approach the discussion from a place of compassion, with the intent to move the coachee forward.

APPENDIX 4 - POWERFUL QUESTIONS

Examples of Descriptive Questions

- What did you notice about...?
- What did you observe about..?
- How would you know...?
- What would be an example of...?
- How does that relate to...?
- Can you describe....?
- What specifically about that....?
- What is different about that vs. _____?

Examples of Creative Questions

- What does that reveal to you?
- What is possible?
- What if you didn't know....?
- What is underneath that?
- What did you discover about...?
- What does that connect you to?
- Who else will you be then?
- What possibilities does that open you to?
- What does that allow?
- If anything were possible?
  If you could have 3 wishes, what would they be?

Questions that support Appreciative Coaching

- Think back to your most positive team experience. What was present?
- Describe a peak experience when working with a team.
- What do you want more of when working with your team?
- Allow yourself to float out to _____(time in the future), what do you notice?
- If anything were possible...what would you want?
- If you could have three wishes, what would they be?

Questions That Promote Somatic Awareness

Body Layer

- Where do you feel that?
- What are you feeling?
- What does that feel like?

Energetic Layer

- Where do you feel that energy?
- Is there an energy blockage?
- What are you noticing about your energy?

Mental/Emotional Layer

- What emotion is coming up?
- If you could experience that objectively, what would you notice?

Intuitive Layer

- What is your "gut feel" about that?
- What does your intuition tell you?
- If anything were possible, what would you tell yourself?

Bliss Layer

- Who are you when you are fully yourself in that situation?
- If there were no restrictions, who would you be?

Awareness Questions

- What would you like to focus on today?
- What would you like to achieve today?
- What would you like to resolve today?
- What do you want?
- What does that mean?
- What does that feel like? Where do you feel it?
- What is important about that to you?
- When were you like that before?
- What's at risk?
- How does that resonate with you?
- What else?
- Does this interaction have a familiar ring to it?
- What is your contribution to this pattern?
- What can you do to stay on course?
- How do you know that?
- What else does that explain?
- Where else do you use that pattern?
- What is important?
- What is most important?
- What is the truth here?
- What is holding you back the most?
- What needs immediate attention?
- If you could see your situation from an observer's position, what would you notice?
- How is this holding you back?
- Is this the key issue?
- Is this the underlying issue?
- Can give you me one specific example of how this issue is affecting you?
- What opportunities are you missing?
- Can you be more specific?
- How specifically does this affect...?
- What do you want to accomplish?
- What outcomes do you want?

Resources Questions

- What do you need?
- How do you need to be?
- Who will you be?
- What resources are available to you?
- What resources do you need?
- What is the biggest challenge you have?
- Really?
- How do you know that?
- How could you simplify that?
- If you had a choice, what would you do?
- What is your biggest fear about that?
- Why are you pushing this so hard?
- What question do you need to ask yourself?
- Is this a need or a want?
- What resource do you need in order to resolve this issue?
- What does your ideal life look like?
- What gets you out of bed each day?
- Do you recall a time when you had that resource?
- What was it like when you fully used that resource?
- If you had that resource in place, how would the issue look/feel now?
- How would having that resource help resolve the issue?
- How would you be different if you had that resource in place?

Action Questions

- What changes can you make moving forward?
- What if nothing changed?
- What is possible?
- Is there another way?
- What is in the way?
- What would need to change in order for this to happen?

- What is the next smallest step you will take?
- Is there anything else you would like to commit to right now?
- How committed are you?
- Do you have the resources to do this?
- What support do you have in place?
- How will you know if that has been successful?

Questions to Uncover Motivations

- What is important to you?
- What do you value?
- Where do you want to be in 5 years? What skills will get you there?
- What do you think you need to work on?
- What assignments are you most interested in?
- How can I best support you?
- What do you need?
- What kind of feedback are you looking for?

BIBLIOGRAPHY

Anderson, Merrill C., *Executive Coaching—The ROI of Building Leadership One Executive at a Time'*

Bench, Marcia, *Career Coaching: An Insider's Guide Second Edition*, Wilsonville, OR, High Flight Press, 2008.

Blake, Amanda, Richard Strozzi-Heckler, Ph.D., and Staci Haines, *Somatics, Neuroscience, and Leadership,* http://www.strozziinstitute.com/

Bolles, Richard N., *What Color is Your Parachute,* Ten Speed Press, Berkeley CA, 2011.

Busche, Gervaise, *Appreciative Inquiry Is Not (Just) About The Positive*, OD Practitioner, Vol. 39, No. 4, pp.30-35, 2007

Coach U, Inc., *The Coach U Personal and Corporate Coach Training Handbook*, New Jersey, John Wiley & Sons, Inc., 2005

Cooperrider, David L., Peter F. Sorensen, Jr., Diana Whitney and Therese F. Yaeger, *Appreciative Inquiry - Rethinking Human Organization Toward a Positive Theory of Change*, Champaign, Illinois, Stipes Publishing, 2000

Covey, Stephen M.R., *The Speed of Trust - One Thing that Changes Everything*, New York, NY, Free Press, 2008

Crane, Thomas G., *The Heart of Coaching,*San Diego, FTA Press, 2009

Dilts, Robert and Judith Delozier, *Encyclopedia of systemic Neuro-Linguistic Programming and NLP New Coding*, 2000

Ellerton, Roger, *Live Your Dreams, Let Reality Catch Up*, Victoria, BC, Trafford Publishing, 2006.

Fairley, Stephen G. and Chris E. Stout, *Getting Started in Personal and Executive Coaching*, New Jersey, John Wiley & Sons, 2004.

Figler & Bolles, *The Career Counsellor's Handbook*, Ten Speed Press, Berkeley CA, 2007.

Flaherty, James, *Coaching - Evoking Excellence in Others*, Jordan Hill, Oxford, Elsevier Butterworth-Heinemann, 2005.

Hammond, Sue, *The Thin Book of Appreciative Inquiry*, Thin Book Publishing Company, 1998.

Hancox, Bob, Russell Hunter and Kristann Boudreau, *Coaching for Engagement*, Vancouver, BC, Tekara, 2010.

Hargrove, Robert, *Masterful Coaching*, San Francisco, CA, John Wiley & Sons, 2008.

Hood, Albert B. and Richard W. Johnson, *Assessment in Counseling - A Guide to the Use of Psychological Assessment Procedures*, Fourth Edition, Alexandria, VA, American Counseling Association, 2007.

Kabat-Zinn, Jon, Ph.D., *Wherever You Go, There You Are - Mindfulness Meditation in Everyday LIfe,* New York, New York, Hyperion, 2005)

Kay, Roselyn and Robyn McCulloch, *Building Capacity for Change: The Power of the Body, AI Practitioner*, ISSN 1741-8224, May 2007.

Lawley, James and Penny Tompkins, *Metaphors in Mind - Transformation Through Symbolic Modeling,* Highgate, London, The Developing Company Press, 2000.

Lipton, Bruce, Ph.D., The Biology of Belief, Unleashing the Power of Consciousness, Matter a& Miracles, Carlsbad, California, Hay House Inc., 2008.

Mehrabian A and SR Ferris, *Inference of Attitudes from Nonverbal Communication in Two Channels,* Journal of Consulting Psychology, 1967 Jun;31(3):248-52.

Morin, Cabrera, *Parting Company, How to Survive the Loss of a Job and Find Another Successfully*, Harcourt Trade Publishers, New York, NY, 2000.

O'Connor, Joseph and John Seymour, *Introducing NLP - Psychological Skills for Understanding and Influencing People*, Hammersmith, London, Element, 1990.

O'Neill, Mary Beth, *Executive Coaching with Backbone and Heart - A Systems Approach to Engaging Leaders with Their Challenges, 2nd Edition*, San Francisco, John Wiley & Sons Inc., 2007

Orem, Sara L., Jacqueline Binkert and Ann L. Clancy, *Appreciative Coaching - A positive Process for Change*, San Francisco, John Wiley & Sons, Inc., 2007

Osterwalder, Alexander and Yves Pigneur, *Business Model Generation*, New Jersey, John Wiley & Sons Inc., 2002

Overdurf, John, *Attention Shifting Coaching*, Atlanta, Georgia, www.overdurf.com

Silsbee, Douglas K., *The Mindful Coach - Seven Roles for Helping People Grow*, Marshall, NC, Ivy River Press, 2007.

Strozzi-Heckler, Richard, *Clairsentience: A Somatic Approach to Intuition*, 2011 Choice Magazine - The Magazine of Professional Coaching, http://www.strozziinstitute.com

Sullivan, Wendy and Judy Rees, *Clean Language - Revealing Metaphors and Opening Minds*, Bethel, CT, Crown House Publishing, 2008.

Underhill, Brian O., Kimcee McNally and John J. Koriath, *Executive Coaching for Results, the Definitive Guide to Developing Organizational Leaders,* San Francisco, CA, Berrett-Koehler Publishers Inc., 2007.

Wahl, Christine, Clarice Scriber and Beth Bloomfield, *On Becoming a Leadership Coach - a Holistic Approach to Coaching Excellence,* New York, NY, Palgrave MacMillan, 2008

Whitney, Diana and Amanda Trosten-Bloom, *The Power of Appreciative Inquiry - A Practical Guide to Positive Change,* San Francisco, Berret-Koehler Publishers, Inc., 2003.

Whitsworth, Laura, Karen Kimsey-House, Henry Kimsey-House and Phillip Sandahl, *Co-Active Coaching*, Nicholas Brealey Publishing, Boston, 2011.

Whitfield, Dwein A., Rich W. Feller and Chris Wood, *A Counselor's Guide to Career Assessment Instruments*, Fifth Edition, Broken Arrow, OK, National Career Developoment Association, 2009.

Wright, Jordan A., *Conducting Psychological Assessment - A Guide for Practitioners*, New Jersey, John Wiley & Sons, 2011.

INDEX

A

Accountability 121
Acknowledgment 168
Action 120, 146
Agreement 143
Appreciative Inquiry 22
Awareness 82, 143

B

Beliefs 156
Blind Spots 85
Body Language 63
Breathing Exercises 70
Bridge Words 107

C

CARA Process 1
Centering 70
Change 47, 73, 102
Confidentiality 73
Connection 61
Criticism 135

E

Emotions 50
Energy 50

F

Feedback 133, 170
Five Layers 45
Follow-Up 126

I

Intention 141
Intuition 42

Printed in Great Britain
by Amazon